THE DREAM OF STAIRS

Also by Susan Noble

Before and After the Darkness
Collected Poems
Drifting Between Empty Tramlines
A Flock of Blackbirds
Inside the Stretch of My Heart

THE DREAM OF STAIRS

A POEM CYCLE

Susan Noble

AESOP Poets
Oxford

AESOP Poets
An imprint of AESOP Publications
Martin Noble Editorial / AESOP
28 Abberbury Road, Oxford OX4 4ES, UK
www.aesopbooks.com

First edition printed privately in 1975.

Second paperback edition published by AESOP Publications
Copyright (c) 2014 The Estate of Susan Noble

The right of the Estate of Susan Noble to be
identified as the author of this work has been
asserted in accordance with sections 77 and 78
of the Copyright Designs and Patents Act 1988.
A catalogue record of this book is available
from the British Library.

Condition of sale:
This book is sold subject to the condition that it shall not, by way of
trade or otherwise, be lent, sold or hired out or otherwise circulated in
any form of binding or cover other than that in which it is published
and without a similar condition including this condition being
imposed on the subsequent purchaser.

ISBN: 978-1-910301-01-2

CONTENTS

Preface	xiii
Publisher's note	xvi
Prologue: To Create	19

PART I   THE HARD ROAD   21

1	*The Hard Road*	23
2	*Apple-Blossom Scent*	24
3	*Quick Birth*	25
4	*Life Story*	26
5	*Nice Child*	27
6	*Cousins*	28
7	*Preview*	29

PART II   CHASTITY   31

8	*Chastity*	33
9	*Grape Picking*	34
10	*Midday*	35
11	*The Rendezvous*	36
12	*First Love*	37
13	*The Ballroom*	38
14	*Falling*	39
15	*Spellbound*	40
16	*Protection*	41

CONTENTS

17	When You Love Someone So Strangely	42
18	When His Arms Closed Around You	43
19	Smile	44
20	The Couple	45
21	The Killing	46
22	Confession	47
23	The Quarrel	48
24	After the Quarrel	49
25	Parting	50
26	Rejection	51
27	The Laughter	52
28	Cut-outs	53
29	Water-Bird	54
30	Cotton-Wool Words	55
31	Separation	56
32	Gift	57
33	Clam	58
34	Chicken Bone	59
35	Spiral of Light	60
36	Wandering Through the Days	61
37	Passing	62
38	Burnt Out by the Shadows	63
39	Facets	64
40	The Aim	65
41	Rope	66
42	The Wedding	67
43	Restoration	68
44	False Image	69
45	Remember	70

PART III THE DREAM OF STAIRS   71

46	*Ballad*	73
47	*Meditation*	74
48	*Duality*	75
49	*The Dream of Stairs*	76
50	*Moon-Treasure*	77
51	*When the Hands Freeze Cold*	78
52	*Lost*	79
53	*Sin*	80
54	*Revelation*	81
55	*Concrete Ground*	82
56	*Neurasthenia*	83
57	*Schizophrenia*	84
58	*Leucotomy*	85
59	*Hospital in Winter*	86
60	*Disillusionment*	88
61	*Percentage*	89
62	*Regret*	90
63	*Change*	91
64	*Onion*	93
65	*Giving*	94
66	*The Madwoman*	95
67	*The Ugly*	97
68	*Blackbird*	98

CONTENTS

PART IV FULCRUM   99

69	Regeneration	101
70	Wakening	102
71	Vision	103
72	The Losing	104
73	See-Saw	105
74	Fulcrum	106
75	Keyboard	107
76	Time Suspended	108
77	Yoga Dance	110
78	The Vision	111
79	Song of a Schizophrenic Monk	112
80	The Singer	113
81	Heat	114
82	Nail Armour	115
83	The Waiting	116
84	Lizard	119
85	Feathers	120
86	Nightmare	121
87	The Bag	122
88	The Open Door	123
89	Illusion	124
90	Nocturne	125
91	Poetry	126
92	Skull-Light	127
93	Selfhood	128
94	Spider	129
95	Interval	130

PART V SHELL   131

96	*Shell*	133
97	*Love*	134
98	*Creation*	135
99	*Fear*	136
100	*Conviction*	137
101	*Being*	138
102	*Energy*	139
103	*Pulse*	140
104	*Continue*	141
105	*Puppet*	142
106	*Nature*	143
107	*Ago*	144
108	*Tunnel*	145
109	*Maternity*	146
110	*No Mother*	147
111	*Development*	148
112	*Release*	149
113	*The Talents*	150
114	*Decision*	151

PART VI WATER   153

115	*Twentieth Century*	155
116	*Individuation*	156
117	*Tryptich*	157
118	*Question*	158

ix

119	*Devils*	160
120	*Duel*	161
121	*Twins*	162
122	*Spur*	163
123	*Holocaust*	164
124	*Conflict*	165
125	*Reclamation*	166
126	*Doubt*	167
127	*Panorama*	168
128	*Corrupt*	169
129	*Black Star*	170
130	*Awakening*	171
131	*Water*	172
132	*Weep Before God, Laugh Before Men*	174
133	*Suicide*	175
134	*Silence*	177

PART VII   THE NINGO PIN   179

135	*Chawton House*	181
136	*She Searched for Happiness*	182
137	*Alien*	183
138	*Afterwards*	184
139	*Shock*	185
140	*To Grieve*	186
141	*Grief*	187
142	*Roses*	188
143	*Return*	189

144	*I Wonder What This Constellation Will Be*	190
145	*Forwards*	191
146	*Resurgence*	192
147	*Gold Door*	193
148	*When the Door Opens*	194
149	*Save This Soul*	195
150	*The Ningo Pin*	196
151	*Inconsolation*	197
152	*The Soul*	198
153	*Waves*	199
154	*Insight*	200
155	*Preserve*	202
156	*Signs*	203
157	*Belief*	204
158	*Evolution*	205
159	*Anchor-man*	206
160	*Reconciliation*	207
161	*Cave God*	208
162	*Knowledge*	209
163	*Security*	210
164	*The Dance*	211
165	*Yellow Flame*	212
166	*Praise*	213
167	*Corn Song*	214

Epilogue: To Speak   215

Index of Poems   217
Index of First Lines   223

Preface

About the book

The Dream of Stairs: A Poem Cycle was privately printed as a posthumous memorial volume in 1975, a year after Susan Noble's untimely death in 1974 at the age of 31.

Having announced with typically light-hearted self-depreciation, 'The muse has struck me!', my sister Susan wrote the poems in batches of half a dozen or more, from 1965 onwards, in what she described as manic bursts of creativity. But these poems are anything but light-hearted, and even a first reading will reveal clearly that levity is not on the menu in a universe 'Where there are no jokes / And people do not pretend.'

Susan's output in the last ten years of her life was prolific, but when it came to compiling the poems, after a good deal of deliberation, a clear thematic structure and underlying development seemed to dictate the final order of that original poignant collection.

To mark the fortieth anniversary of Susan's death, this second edition, published in hardback, paperback and Kindle, makes the book publicly available for the first time. There are a number of changes to the first edition: a slight reordering of the poems, minor amendments to the structure of the poem cycle, a revised, enhanced layout, and indexes of titles and first lines.

More significantly, the original selection has been augmented by many additional poems, which clearly fit within the cycle thematically and structurally.

Five companion volumes are also being published: *Inside the Stretch of My Heart* and *Before and After the Darkness* are two previously unpublished collections of poems; *Collected Poems*, which incorporates all three poetry collections in one comprehensive volume; *A Flock of Blackbirds* (selected novellas and short stories); as well as the novel, *Drifting Between Empty Tramlines*.

PREFACE

Profits from the sales of all six volumes are being donated to three charities: Mind, the Samaritans and Sane. For more details, see page xvi.

Facsimiles of the original typescripts and manuscripts are available online at

www.aesopbooks.com/susannoble

Martin Noble
Oxford, 2014

About the author

Brought up in South London, my sister, Susan Noble, was the second of three children. Her childhood was enriched by being part of our large and closely-knit Jewish family. Unfortunately stricken by polio (then known as infantile paralysis) in her early years, Susan went through life with a degree of physical handicap which she was to overcome with courage and determination.

Educated at Croydon High School, Susan studied English at Somerville College, Oxford. After graduating, Susan worked in London, first at the Royal National Institute for the Blind, dictating books for transcription into Braille, and later at the National Central Library in London, where she qualified as a Chartered Librarian.

Susan's exceptional sensitivity was reflected in the prolific outpouring of poems that make up *The Dream of Stairs* and *Inside the Stretch of My Heart*. In these intense, haunting poems, she chronicles her personal response to the world around her, while vividly portraying the inner landscape of her mental and emotional struggle.

Judith Frankel
Netanya, 2014

PREFACE

Susan Noble

One's first impression of Susan was of fragility. She was an acutely sensitive person, but her physical and emotional fragility really masked a very great spiritual strength.

Her sensitivity indeed was not directed only towards herself, but towards others. She was sensitive to the needs of others, and her strength and also perhaps some of her inner conflicts came from a deep desire for goodness which could not be matched in reality by the world as she found it.

Susan passionately wished to be independent; she struggled for it from the time she went to university, and throughout her work as a librarian, and she was able to maintain it to the very end.

There was an intellectual and emotional intensity which burned within her and which predominantly found outward expression in her writing and when she expressed herself thus she did so with great imaginative power and also with an uncompromising honesty and integrity.

The late Rabbi Dr David Goldstein
South London, July 1974

Publisher's note

All profits from the sale of this volume
are being donated to the following charities:

The National Association for Mental Health
www.mind.org.uk

www.samaritans.org

www.sane.org.uk

THE DREAM OF STAIRS

Prologue: To Create

A poem cannot be contrived wilfully,
But grows out of a black knot;
The sharp needle unravels the tangled lump
Into a long thread of the imagination,
Which can be cut into shreds
Or resolved into a tight knot once again.

PART I

THE HARD ROAD

THE DREAM OF STAIRS

1   *The Hard Road*

You have chosen the hard road,
The hard road and the steep hill,
Where there are no jokes
And people do not pretend.

You have chosen the stretching rack,
Where there is no sofa to sink into,
No easy way out,
And no crutch of creed to rest upon.

You see the daylight,
White and sometimes silvery,
But most of the time grey, greylight,
You have chosen the hard road.

2 *Apple-Blossom Scent*

Apple-blossom scent,
Sickly strong,
Sends me hurtling through the tunnel of time
To a class in a college common-room ten years ago.
Long wooden table, unvarnished, raw.
Twelve girls, mushroom faces, straight hair,
Cold on a summer's day.
Green quadrangle through the window,
Dons drifting past
In twos and threes
After a meeting.
Locked in a bottle of air, apple-blossom scent,
I cannot understand the silent thinking of the faces
Motionless around the table.
Contemptuous, I want to escape into the sunlight.
But now that the years have passed a new decade,
I find that these girls have run away
In different directions,
And I am still seeking too late to recapture
The thinking, which I forgot to do
In my adolescence.

3 *Quick Birth*

Reality painful
As gasping fish out of water
Breathes
Fills its lungs
Crying
Shapes
Of colour and sound and blurred
Movements
From warmth of waters
Into sharp-edged air

4 Life Story

Born to a bellow of music outside the hospital window,
The nurse consoled my mother, 'It's only a sousaphone.'
My mother was soothed, but I was not.
And as the years passed by,
I roared in anger at every passing image.
Slowly the music turned into waves of acceptance,
Crotchet upon quaver, staccato surprise.
And now I wait in silence for the next chord.

5 *Nice Child*

When I was a child, a naughty child,
I watched the nice little girl play with her hair-ribbon.
She wore a lemon and white gingham dress
Of glazed cotton,
And her plaits were looped into glazed yellow bows.
Her forehead was large and serene
As she sat on the carpet quietly thinking.
When I was a child, I wanted to be that nice little girl,
And now against my will, it seems,
I have changed into what she was,
And when a thought passes through my mind
I filter it with pursed lips.
Is this a change for the better
Or do I no longer exist?

6 *Cousins*

Cousins
Are siblings once removed and hover between
The fence of friendship
And the telepathic silence of blood-bondage,
Puppet figures, that assert their distance,
And fall back in a quick glance
To the common patterns two generations ago.
An echoed laugh, twin chortles will surprise
In the face of alien accents, opposite gestures.
Only the curve of the thumb against the palm
Reminds us that we are falling away from the old stencil
And our children's children will stare at each other
Like strangers.

7   *Preview*

The first time I glimpsed Hell
Was on a Sunday afternoon,
Lounging on the red velveteen sofa.
The radio blared a gospel sermon,
That to neglect this message was black.
There was no turning back,
And the sofa changed to a sea of waves,
Tiny stinging ants probing the corrupted corpse,
Grey tongues of water lashing eternally.
The cat on the cushion by my feet purred
And washed her face
With the side of a grey paw,
The fur grown old from years of running up and down
In no particular direction,
Whichever way her energy disposed.
The yellow bow round her neck curved
In mock strangulation,
But she continued to purr a telephone buzz,
Reassuring in its regularity.
The first time I glimpsed Hell
Was only for a moment,
And afterwards I listened to the afternoon play
In front of the electric fire
And read the colour supplement in the glowlight,
Reassured by the artificial coals.

PART II

CHASTITY

8   *Chastity*

I am pale and white
Calm and quiet
Cool and bright.
What has never known never wants
And what has never wanted never needs.
I know there is a realm beyond my sphere
And what is unexperienced can lead to fear.
I fear and want not, want and fear not,
Know that I don't have and have what I don't know.
Day comes and is bright and light,
Night comes and is dark and black.
Day I know – night I know not.
Come hither – come not.
Cool and bright
Calm and quiet
I am pale and white.

9   *Grape Picking*

Slowly the sweet-sour juice trickling
From the spilled cluster
Is sucked up by the hot grass beneath the vines.
The sun is flat and hot on our covered heads.
The windowing vine-leaves protect
The heads of the grape bunches
Which peep out unaware of the midday heat.
The work is slow and rhythmic yet full of complications.
This bunch is second-grade so must be discarded.
The sabra-girl is fat and copper in the sunlight.
The grapes are sweet and bursting in the bushes.

10 *Midday*

Discovered
Sucking slowly on a straw
Gazing at the rosebush in the park,
Thinking of the colours, not of the bottle in my hand,
I blushed as he walked past,
Caught in the act
Remnant of babyhood.
He could never know the thought process,
Analysis of the trembling leaves
Curved downwards, rubbery oil-like surface,
Twitching greenery as the breeze flickers past,
Vulnerable to each vibration
Just as I am,
In his sight, a fool regressed
To slow sucking on a straw alone in a lunch-hour park.

11   *The Rendezvous*

His moccasins spattered with green mud of Chelsea,
Sardonically smiling with elegant sweetness
About to encounter the girl of his wanting,
Who is young and spry,
Graceful with eyelids enchanting.
The sand-dunes are sinking,
The sand-dunes are sinking,
Make love while you're young
And leave later your thinking.

They eat in a delicate Indian tea-place,
A well-chosen meal with some tentative chatter.
She's tongue-tied and pausing, but it does not matter,
The cigarette smoke counteracts the cool silence.
The sand-dunes are sinking,
The sand-dunes are sinking,
Make love while you're young
And leave later your thinking.

12 *First Love*

All that summer
The trees cracked into triangles,
The sunlight over the fences.
She waited for his letters.
Two lines were enough
For the words to dance like ants.
Along the streets people in silent cauls
Broke through into smiles.
The campus was littered with waving arms.
Fish in the sea,
Fluorescent,
Leaping silver,
Remember always.

13   *The Ballroom*

Lilting and loving, loving and lilting,
The music is playing, the flowers are wilting,
The ballroom is heated, the lightbulbs are fizzing,
I'm whirling and twirling, now spinning and dizzy.
Nothing is static, all's mobile and busy.
My partner's refilling the wineglass I'm tilting.
Lilting and loving, loving and lilting.
I'm dizzy, I'm spinning, my wine is o'erspilling,
The music is frisky and happy and trilling,
Willing us to dance and we are so willing.
Lilting and loving, loving and lilting.

14 *Falling*

The falling in love down through a hole in the heart
Through the bubbling blood, that bounces,
Day after day,
On a hope, that may come to nothing.
Daisy chain, will he, won't he?
White petals grow around the yellow pollen,
Will never stop curling,
Petal-points moist in the sunlight.
Can never stop loving.

15 *Spellbound*

This hypnotist
Has a sandalwood voice
That cracks in the middle and vibrates
Like layers of brown leather.
There is a blackness in his laugh,
In his prune eyes and beetle brows.
I am not afraid, simply magnetised.
The air around him hangs with violet dust,
Pulling me outwards, far away
To bluebells growing in a wood, prickly in the spring,
Beneath crackling branches
And then deep down, down
To the gloom of a hut in winter,
A light shining flat upon the ceiling,
Onto a body asleep.
There is pain here and some apprehension.
His voice crackles, buzzes into my ear,
The light is bright, two tiny specks in his eyes,
Now blue, now purple,
Glassy curve of iris.
The bluebells in the wood smell of sandalwood.
I want to stay here, here in this violet pool,
Drunk with submission,
Compelled to rest within the two tiny speckles
Gleaming from the very pit of his apprehension.

16 *Protection*

To be loved
Is to stop thinking.
Lampposts, restaurants, trees
Gaze back admiringly.
Barriers are crushed all around.
Skin pores stretch, take gulps of afternoon air,
Hair sways,
Nonchalance of the swinging breeze.

17 *When You Love Someone So Strangely*

When you love someone so strangely
That to stretch out through the air
Is to crack the tree-trunks into splintering thongs,
The ground is shattered into a thousand cracks
And the white sky falls down on top of your head,
A woolly weight from which there is no escape.
If you could reach him at this moment in time
And sink within the squeezing ventricles of his heart,
You would become his blood and bone.
There is no unity possible,
No way to evade the cut of pain as he walks
Away down the pavement,
A black figure ambling into the distance,
Out of sight and entering a new pattern of time
Beyond the blurred edge of your shadow.

18 *When His Arms Closed Around You*

When his arms closed around you,
Warm peace of dovelike knowing,
Rocking-chair haven of flesh,
You were cut off from the turbulence of life
With the rubber-edged knife;
And the morning after
Your fingernails scraped away
The numb dust of white palms
Into daylight.

Myopically I see him only at close range,
His thoughts, glances,
The grim thinking of his mouth, corners turned down.
Large eyes, black, anxiously they watch.
He fingers a yellow sideburn.
Envious, I hear the other discuss him as a person
In restaurants and theatres,
This dining-room, that party,
But I am trapped by my vision, almost a pointillism.
Grain upon grain I see, pore upon pore,
A magnifying glass to enlarge every gesture.
Which of us is right?

19 *Smile*

'Why do you smile all the time,' he asked,
'That stupid smile? What does it mean?'
'I see the discrepancy, the irony of things.'
'Stop observing and try to feel.
You have no feelings, no feelings of your own.'
He thumped his hand against his knee.
Black beard jerked against the corner of the mantelpiece
In the background.
'Yes, I do feel, but I observe as well,
And the difference between the two makes me laugh.'
She giggled, unable to stop, and swayed to and fro.
'Go on laughing,' he said. 'Laugh as much as you like.
Laugh and laugh and laugh.'
She laughed and laughed
And laughed and laughed again.
And then she felt that there was nothing left to laugh at,
So she stopped and sighed with the weight of loneliness.
He stared at her, satisfied.
And his face relaxed into a flicker of a ghost of a smile.
And they became acquainted with one another.

20 *The Couple*

You lay above me, cutting off the blue
Thick slice of sky that tried participation
In our secret individual conversation,
But I ignored the sky and wanted only you.

The time hung archetypal, slow and true,
For nations full have known the peace and pride,
When man and woman slumber side by side
Multitudes since and centuries ago.

The blue sky crumpled brown in jealous whim
And rain burst down upon us, pricking cold,
And purged us of our wisdom aeons old
And I was cold again, still loving him.

21 *The Killing*

He mocked her drawing,
Black criss-crossed edges of ink overlapping
To form a half-smile portrait.
He found the composition banal,
Which she had carefully fitted
Into the afternoon shade.
And when in recompense he admired
Her glow of rusty hair, long cheekbone,
She felt no pride, but changed unwittingly
Into a child, placated
Too late.

22 *Confession*

We sat in the damp evening air,
Soaking in the green grass.
The firm press of the park-bench.
Far out on all sides trees and white sky
And the cold vacuum of September
Stretching out, no barriers, no future.
At that moment, gust of wind
Against the mouldering ground,
We confessed our fear,
The fear of the surging crowds
And the things that cannot be understood,
The dwindling away of love and the sting
Of a wasp probing further and further,
And between us there grew a bond not of affection,
But the steel halter that straps two children together
As they freeze in their beds on a black November night
And listen to the monotonous creak of the rocking chair
As it shudders in the wind.

23 The Quarrel

They didn't mean to quarrel.
It just happened,
Crackling sun pressing down their hair,
Burning their necks, melting their fingers into dampness.
She disliked his accent.
His mistrusted her frivolity.
The quarrel cracked between them
Like a nut
And they were left to chew over the fragments,
Spitting out the splinters of woody shell,
That were lodged within it,
Blushing at their own coarseness,
Regressed to childhood
Squabbling.

24 After the Quarrel

After the quarrel
We sat in the night-blackened room
The curtains drawn open
Onto the rain outside.
It fell quickly in liquid pincers,
Slicing up the stones.
The branches trembled like spiders,
Grown old from years of steady rootage
And the clouds were drained green,
Exhausted by the downpour.
We sat and waited, as the furniture in the room
Grew white from the concrete yard outside,
Reflected through the blurred glass,
Whiteness like streaks of old salt.

25 *Parting*

If we never see each other again,
A sensible snipping away, which may perhaps happen
According to the slow blow of time
That has been dragging us down into a black quicksand,
Then I will be reconciled.
It will not be an easy chopping
Nor a simple conclusion to an old bond,
For here was no spell that held us down,
Except the quick sparring of minds at ease
Turbulent against the forces of life
That found sometimes a silent peace
Under the gold evening glow
When words had petered away
And had thrown us back
Into some past world long ago
Where we had been unified,
Black shadows downwards
Into the peace of the cave.
If we never see each other again,
Then I will be reconciled.
For some strange ebony wing brought us together
To lash one another with the fury of polarity
Until we merged into a surprised similarity
And now it is time for us to flow away again
Back into separation.

26 *Rejection*

I have wilfully flicked an ounce of flesh
Off his back with my Shylock knife.
I will not be dissuaded by drooping glances
Or the firm, door-blocking stance.
But leave straight away
With blinkered stare-ahead indifference
And wonder later why I feel no remorse
For a deed that was not unjust.

27 *The Laughter*

The laughter grew
Into gold coils.
It fizzled up the dark hours,
As fish grin in flashes
Around a weed
Deeply embedded
Within roots of mud and stone.
It eclipsed the sun,
That would have shone black
In the knowledge of what cannot be resolved,
As layer upon layer
Is peeled away
In the atomic dazzle at dawn.
The laughed clanged sombrely.
It re-echoed and burnt away the apprehensions,
That had bound us together
And we were soldered into one dead golden ring.

28 *Cut-outs*

When we met,
Cardboard figures
From a children's game,
I could not penetrate beneath
The quiet stance and watchful hostility;
And when six months later the surface was shattered,
I wanted to retrieve the wasted hours of polarity
And could not reach close enough,
As I clung on to those firm shoulders
Like a child soothed to sleep after a storm.

29 *Water-Bird*

Parabola of water.
Hoop bent together mischievously,
The left curve a smooth line of white,
And the right curve snipped off into droplets,
Bouncing against the water-coated concrete with a smash,
Painful spurts out in all directions
Into sharp water-spikes.
A hopping bird nearby nibbles the residue of water
With its beak,
Chewing the jumping lumps of white liquid,
Wings flutter, frantically
Shivering,
Longs to be rubbed dry, caressed into warmth,
But instead flaps around the concrete for two minutes
To raise the blood level,
So that it can hop under the dripping parabola again
And nibble lumps of water.

30 *Cotton-Wool Words*

Cotton-wool words,
Cloud-spun, cloud-spun,
A whirling white ball of candy-floss.
Words that do not echo you,
Words that do not echo me.
Let them consume themselves in cannibalism
And the air will speak between us.

31 *Separation*

Our love, fulfilled, would not be so.
Better to separate us between rows
Of houses, wall after wall,
Like a pack of trick cards,
Carefully assembled.
To join us would send the pack
Flying over into a heap.
Thinking of you,
I focus my attention upon a patch of wallpaper,
Cream and gold panels jutting out
From a white background,
Thick woolly paper,
If speared with a blade it would sag
And tear into a feathered edge,
The knife point lodged within the brittle plaster
Would scratch a shower of chalky crumbs,
The illusion of gold quietly explained.
Seldom we see each other from year,
Only a glimpse,
Your retreating figure down a side-street,
Face on a bus in profile, immobile in thought,
Through a buzz of conversation,
A flicker of laughter,
Echoes of a bond.
It survives eagerly,
Anticipating the impossible.

32 *Gift*

No security is possible, gateway to your love.
I cannot banish the fear of the door closed in my face
On a winter's afternoon at four o'clock ebb-tide,
Black gates iron-strong against the white sky.
No promises can ever give me
The golden sea of oblivion,
Anaesthetising the cut of the wind.
Only by your sudden whim,
When all the world is flattened to a concrete slab
And no thought-shadows flicker across my mind,
Do I glimpse the wave of love in your probing eyes.

33 *Clam*

You know I feel for you,
Your every motion.
Your look darts hatred at their empathy,
Which draws me beneath your skin
Into the marrow of your bones
To find strength in your hesitations.
I see your eyes blink black and narrow
Against the watchful grey of my glance.
I cannot detach it, snip it away,
Quick flip of elastic boomerang,
Only wish to remain a clam-parasite for ever.

34   *Chicken Bone*

I could tear you out of me,
Chicken bone swallowed and gone down the wrong way
To choke me continually;
And sometimes when the breath returns, I feel your love,
Eyes mobile, gazing hard,
And then the choking begins again.
I cannot decide whether the bone is an injury to my body
Or whether it is the spur
That keeps me gasping for more breath.

35 *Spiral of Light*

Knowing how he does not love you,
You fall through the side of a mountain,
Ribcage of rocks
Will open,
When all other ways are barred.
When Adam gave Eve his rib,
He grew unmanned, exultant.
In this there is no giving.
Now you wait for the darkness to trample,
Abate.
Leaving a spiral of light
White as shining eyes,
That beg you to accept
All imperfections.

36 *Wandering Through the Days*

Wandering through the days
With you lodged in my heart.
Explosion of living difference
Beaten into flesh.
I count the moments
Of no-clock time
Until the mirror will turn silver
With surprise.

37 *Passing*

Standing in the black rain
By the mud-wet bicycle,
Curve of steel glistening
Beneath the light of the shop-façade
I saw him approach,
Beanpole tall against the horizontal of the kerbside
And the flattened car-tops that zoomed by,
Lamp-post silhouette, that hovered against my own,
And willed me to speak.
Mud silence filled my mouth,
Clodded up my ears and stuffed my throat
With numb invisibility.
Slowly his shadow loped past,
Jutting upwards,
Leaving me diminished, squat,
Crunched flat as the car-tops that zoomed by.

38 *Burnt Out by the Shadows*

Our friendship came to nothing, petered away,
Not by a quarrel,
But burnt out by the shadows
Of the room, where we sat
And could not bridge the gap,
Because of your pride, my subservience.
It echoed in my mind, yawning over the years.
Now on a September evening,
Six o'clock in the flickering twilight,
We collide at the corner of a street.
The buzzing traffic, the click of passing shoppers
Roll away the differences between us,
And there is only a white stretch of pavement
And an airy smile.

39 *Facets*

Please believe
That I want nothing more from you,
Nothing at all,
And if you disbelieve this.
Then know, at least, that you
Are under no obligation to give it.
The years have plaited thread between us,
And trapped within our web other lives.
They have filtered away the things
That we believed in long ago
Before the age of complexity began.
Who can recognise the truth any more
Of a word, of a psalm, of an idea,
As layer upon layer is peeled away
With an awareness of reality so vivid
That it negates itself, having lost the conflict
Of surprised consciousness?
So I can only say to you again,
Please believe
That I want nothing more from you,
Nothing at all,
And if I did want it,
How would I know whether the wanting was a real wish,
Or a wanting of a wanting,
Or a wanting to be wanted?

40 *The Aim*

You can try
For a minute, for an hour, for a year,
To win his love, her love.
Stony defences thrown your efforts back
Jakari-like into your face,
And your features. blunted by denial,
Do not fit together any more.
Then on a sunny day in a crowd,
Unthinking, unwanting, uncalculating, you smile
As you step off the kerb,
And realise that a lifetime's exertions can come to nothing
And a face smiles back.
Whose face? It does not matter.
The dart has hit the bullseye by mistake.
It is not gratitude that you feel,
Only surprise,
Wry acceptance.

41 *Rope*

High above the earth
Upon a tightrope
A man and a woman
Step away the days
High and straight as the crow flies.
He will not hold her hand
Ruthless the gap between their wrists
Clenched to exertion
Far below the snow is flaked into layers of whiteness
Caught upon the mounds of the hillsides
And the sky is as black as a gleaming tin-can.
Silk
Of breath and snow and sky,
Silk of skin sinking into terror,
Ankle over ankle upon the rope.
There are no milestones,
No cuts to totem the pole,
To tell of the days
That remain to be stayed.
Some love there will be
Between the man and the woman
And the stepping over will go on,
Over and on.

42 *The Wedding*

Ten years ago they sat together at a wedding.
She smiled across the table, excluding him,
Smug and secure in her pink satin.
She nibbled prawns, a gleaming silver fork,
Plump arms waving, perfume and the band.
She laughed aloud. Confident she saw
Everything in black and white,
While he hovered foolishly in the background,
Hesitated,
Seeing the stripes, the grey.

And now he walks past her in the street,
Long strides, heedless.
And she hesitates, seeing the grains, the shadows.
But he has forgotten her completely,
A vacant doll,
And she must bear the double lash
Of total daylight
And his ignorance.

43 *Restoration*

Can it ever be recovered,
Integrity of childhood?
Bird nibbling cherry in the hay,
Wisps of yellow grass beneath the hot sun,
Restored to the old, old frozen self.
Snowflakes dripping down the silk of cheeks
On a January morning.
All is swept away by the brush of love,
Yellow flame burns away the dust
And leaves a new face,
Burnished with understanding.

44 *False Image*

Crossing the road,
I thought I recognised a familiar face,
A mistake,
Which caused the face to split in two,
The face of a stranger nonchalantly aloof
And the face of a friend in open communication,
And as we passed the island in the middle
It switched itself into a different key,
Aware that it had to fit an unknown pattern
And recognising itself from my surprise
Where I was aware of this imposition,
Erased from those features the old remembered shadows,
Leaving the scrubbed detachment of a stranger.

45 *Remember*

At the end of the long day,
When the leaves of the oak-trees rattle,
And sleepy officer-workers march home
In twos and threes,
I remember the sabra-boy with the guitar,
Blue shirt and spade of ginger beard,
Thick features stretched into a grin,
Rattle of whining music.
The scratch of cat gut, the blur of discords,
The cry of our ancestors in the ghettoes,
Before they left the pogroms for an alien way of life.
The leaves rattle
And the guitar slurs.
The roaring traffic blurs with the scream
Of generations ago,
Crying, dying in heaps,
A yellow scarf spotted with blood
And a pair of stiff leather shoes
Thrown down a flight of stairs
By an old woman in black
With hollow cheekbones of stone.
At the end of the long day
The leaves rattle
And I remember the sabra-boy with the guitar.

PART III

THE DREAM OF STAIRS

46   *Ballad*

I wish, I wait. I wait and I wish.
The fish swims a flick in the sparkling pool.
I know, I hope. I hope and I know
That life is both gentle, both gentle and cruel.

The wind moans, it murmurs. It murmurs and moans.
The fish swims a flick in the sparkling pool.
I wonder, I ponder. I ponder and wonder
That life is both gentle and cruel.

He came, he went. He went and he came.
The fish swims a flick in the sparkling pool.
I linger, I hunger. I hunger and linger,
For life is both gentle and cruel.

He loved, he loathed. He loathed and he loved
The fish swims a flick in the sparkling pool.
I tremble, I sorrow. I sorrow and tremble.
For life is both gentle and cruel.

I accept, I rebel. I rebel and accept.
The fish swims a flick in the sparkling pool.
I marvel, I suffer. I suffer and marvel,
For life is both gentle and cruel.

47 *Meditation*

Take a petal, imprint it on your mind
And you have reached a point of meditation:
It sounds too simple, dangerous and strong
To undergo this odd initiation.
For very soon all unity is broken
By fragments of bright individuation:
A flashing light, a noise, a sudden motion
And you have split the mood of elevation
And trickled from the cup of the sublime
Into the aching prickles of finite time.
Away from the glorious calmness of the static
Into the painful turbulence of the dramatic.
Those who seek the clarity of unity
As opposed to the dimness of community
Will find it in a leaf, a star, a tree,
A sudden glimpse of deep serenity.
Take a petal, imprint it on your mind
And you have reached a point of meditation:
It sounds too simple, dangerous and strong
To undergo this odd initiation.

48 *Duality*

On each shoulder is perched an object.
On my right a dazzling glob of silver
Reflects the world around in microcosm,
Passing faces, a door blown open, the petal of a daisy,
Crystallised into gleaming speckles for ever.
On my left a black and craggy lump,
Opaquely jutting out,
A barrier between myself and the sky,
Looks like coal, but something more insidious,
Sinister shades,
A wilful turning away from the light,
Could be evil, could be an outreaching.

49 *The Dream of Stairs*

A wide expanse of gleaming spirals ripple
Once carved in agony out of human bone.
I hesitate to touch the toothlike ladder.
It greets me with a hideous white leer.
I crumple all my fear into a ball
And tiptoeing high I throw it all aloft.
It swoops clean to the top of the bony height
And flutters down again, a wispy boomerang.
I must awake and breathe the living day.

I kick the ball about on the crumbling ground.
It yoyos happily from side to side
And I am left to bear my feet intact.
I quickly start to climb the grinning stairs.
They groan at every step and softly mutter,
With grinding teeth and cold conspiracy.
I must awake and breathe the living day.

50 *Moon-Treasure*

At the back of the moon,
Beyond the green cheese
Lies a bad of black ash,
Love never spoken,
Killed by schedule,
Split and sprouting,
Tramples over the black craters,
Wailing, eerie,
Stampedes on all fours,
Growing spiders,
Scream of the wind.
Do not stare too long at the moon
Or you will turn to green cheese.

51 *When the Hands Freeze Cold*

Everyone must bear between their fingers
Icy rods of fear
When the hands freeze cold
At night the black pools of the netherworld
Pull us down
By day the flashing chaos screams in all directions
Stretching us into a Catherine wheel
Of turbulence.

52 *Lost*

Over the hills,
Olive-black trees and wet sky at night,
My voice broke free,
Screaming after the running dog,
Legs rolled up and down in the damp soil,
Like sausages on a machine
And the grass started to revolve
Around and around,
Burning shrieks,
While the black fur darted away behind the leaves.
The sky turned to rubber,
Soft upon the trees swaying,
And the mud of the path sank willingly
Beneath my feet,
A murderous life-shaft,
Released from the cords of day and night.
I screamed and screamed and screamed
Until my voice was flying around the trees
And the night filled my lungs like wet leaves.

53 *Sin*

In the falling away,
Grey wings of bird cloud downwards from the sky,
Lies the separation, wings parting wilfully
From the One Source of Being;
Resting sky high.
Long ago could not see Him, being a part of the whole
Evaporated unity and could feel no pain of
Selfhood cramping limits, fallen, fallen away.
Now from this level the space hangs above and below,
And each bird hovers at a different height,
Conjoined to none.
But if the wings should fail, surprise clipping,
Flapping terror,
Quick spin around to grope at fingers of air,
And to fall, fall through the blue vacuum,
Pricking particles of light,
Drifting deeper to I know not where.

54 *Revelation*

When I tore away the curtain of my pretences,
And saw myself face to face,
No shining spirit,
But dust and flesh and dust,
I realised that my old soul had been a lie.

Naked recognition
Does not come smoothly
But grates upon the longing,
The wish to climb higher.
Only by this quick tearing away into skinless agony
Can I begin the slow ascent uphill.

55 *Concrete Ground*

Cold clatter of feet against the pavement.
Empty grey concrete in the square askew.
When I have stepped over this line
And this one, and this one,
Dizzy succession of cuts upon the stone,
I will have accepted the pain,
The long pain of the endless ground.
Empty space despite the criss-crossed blocks,
The squares that do not fit,
The cracks, the jutting-out pieces of stone,
Upon which I trip.
Whose fault?
Stone, cold stone.
Grey merging into white.
When I have stepped upon this line,
Foot flat across it,
Dissected into two and joined again
By the fragments of stone,
Then will I know
The endless pain.

56 *Neurasthenia*

Virginia saw it too,
The door of the lounge opening sharply
And a crowd of smoke jostling people,
Rose in a vase on the sideboard,
The bald man's moustache glistening with beer,
A mouth opening and shutting with laughter,
Removed from its face.
Dizziness as the colours clash
And scream around my ears.
I do not know which way to move.

57 Schizophrenia

The book of my mind lies open
And the left page, the inner world, leads into
The right page of the outer world;
But my book has been chopped in half
And I can only read
The insular left page.

58　*Leucotomy*

They cut a slice out of the brain,
Triangle of water melon,
Swift removal before the computer had managed
To find the right program.
Strange jumble of nerves;
What cannot be understood
Should never be anaesthetised,
But must be endured,
If not by stoicism
Then let the old, slow white days drift past
In obedience to the click of time
And the rise and fall
Of the electrical mind.

59 *Hospital in Winter*

The snow is falling February white
Outside the hospital window,
On a church-bells Sunday afternoon.
Voices.

Will my mother come to visit me?
Won't my mother come to visit me?
My addled brain swoops to the circles of snowflakes.
I see Hell besmattered against the window-pane,
Besmattered against my face, my pain.

Whispering voices are telling me something, telling me.
Please be quiet, I can't hear what you're saying.
A word. Stuck on a word,
A word going round and around.
'Even. Evie. Even.' What does it mean? 'Even. Evie.'

A coal fire is burning in the centre of the long wall,
And a girl is reading a book slumped in an old armchair,
Pink dressing-gown and lanky hair over long shoulders.
She turns round to stare at the door,
A bony face, the face of a horse.

THE DREAM OF STAIRS

My frozen feet. Rows of white beds stretching far out
On either side of me.
Are there people in the beds? I cannot see them.
Are there people outside the window?
I cannot hear them, but I can hear voices,
A crowd of voices
Screaming outside this castle window, a battle-scene.
Snowflakes and church-bells. Perhaps it is Easter.
No, it is too early.
Not yet time for the white Easter Sunday.

Nobody will come to visit me
Snowflakes falling.

60 *Disillusionment*

I have scrubbed the house from top to bottom,
Sponged away the dust and dirt,
The balls of hair and the cobwebs
With a steaming cloth of acid,
And peeled away the paintwork by mistake.
Germless,
Inoffensive,
Non-idiosyncratic,
And I wish I had not done it.

61 *Percentage*

So many gaps,
White patches, which I should have painted
And words I should have spoken.
The morning after
The mind serves to redress the balance
By filling in the loopholes and the crevices,
So that in reflection
The memory is unified, perfected.
To accept a life of fifty per cent is difficult.
To think in totality is impossible.
Somewhere between I throw a coil
And lasso together the fragments with the whole.
A release of energy as polar opposites are conjoined.
An explosion of atoms into the mushroom fallout
Of realisation.

62 *Regret*

Cut out with regret,
Pull back into the basket of the womb,
Kill with a light speedier than time,
That turns somersault
And undoes in a cartwheel of breech birth
What should never have grown to flame.
A love grew
Weighty with surprise.
It burnt away contentment,
It made vulnerable the perception,
Which used to measure by hours,
But now calculates in gripped recollections.
Cut out with regret,
Kill with a light speedier than time,
What should never have grown to flame.

63 *Change*

The girl with the operated nose
Walks along the city street,
Smiles thankyou to the glances
At the beauty which she does not own
And wonders whether she would rather
Be herself again and alone.
Drills drumming along the crowded streets,
As buildings are operated upon by cranes,
Milling crowds weave through the scaffolding,
Dodging this way and that,
And all is subject to change.
A falling ladder and a heap of bricks
Could crush her bones to disfigurement,
And the change would seem a natural law.
Why then this guilt at the slither of bone
Peeled away by a surgeon's knife?
The tiny scars on the skin barely visible
Throb in her head,
An echo of the scars to her loving self,
Which the old face inflicted.

A year ago today,
I walked down the streets alone,
White pavements on all sides and no-one smiled.
The frosty sun tingled against the shop windows
And weeds sprung up round the trees in the damp soil.
I could see the cord, that strung the weeds to the sun,
And I could hear a thundering silence, lingering peace.
Today the streets are crowded,
Bobbing bodies, laughing lips,
Sentences shuffle in the air
And a street accordion vibrates against the window-pane,
But I have lost the cord, that bound the weeds to the sun,
And I cannot see the damp soil
Or hear the thundering silence.

64 *Onion*

I have peeled off the façade,
Wrenching off the onion-skin brown wrapping,
Crisp tatters
And the trickling flesh beneath
Makes me want to cry.
Perhaps with each passing year I shall shed a new skin,
Caterpillar rhythm,
Sporadic stretching.
Only nine lives are given.
Should a core be found beneath the white rings,
Will it be myself
Integer?

65 *Giving*

Can never give enough,
As much as I would wish
Of myself to others.
Convoluted umbrella
I point to apex,
The utmost of effort,
The peak I seek
Daily,
But never reach.
Invisible gap of steel,
Slice between magnet and knife,
Before they jump together and touch,
Cannot be pierced without dangerous
Fusion.

66   *The Madwoman*

There is a madwoman gaunt and brown
Sitting by the carriage door,
Her hair is lank, her eyes are dull.
Her cheekbones hollow, her clothes are poor.
Sitting by the carriage door.
Soon she moves to make room for more.

We pass a suburb, it flickers by,
Time flickers by and smoke flickers by,
And through the wisps of its dusky glow
She begins to show signs of a strange elation,
Unusual and manic, an elevation,
Static, ecstatic, the joy of madness,
The joy of meaningless contemplation.
It has no meaning, no rational meaning,
And is unrelated to external location.
It just follows the rhythm of her own metabolism,
Up and down. The train slows down,
And we have arrived at our destination.

The train slows down and the smoke drifts by.
The woman is quiet and calm as before,
Lank and bleak and gaunt and poor.
Is it vapid sentimentality
Or even the sign of a low mentality
To sympathise were her ebb and flow?
This unsophisticated joy.
Manic and pure,
Meaningless and sure,
Simple to the core.

67 *The Ugly*

Let the ugly speak
In angular smiles,
Distorted glances.
Let them express in a grin of separated teeth
The warmth
That disturbs their ill-matched features
Into a symmetry
Of reconciliation.

68 Blackbird

Frozen fingernails turning yellow.
Cold shivers around my shoulder blades.
On a bench in the square,
Legs crossed in beige trousers,
An aeroplane above against the sky,
And in the vacuum between the ground
And my dangling shoe
A blackbird walks on spindly legs,
Scratches its wing, feathers ruffled into a tremble,
Like the cascading notes of a harmonium,
The fluttering ceases and it looks up at me curiously,
Pointed beak upturned like a child.
I could stamp my shoe on it,
Stamp out the trembling before it knew the moment,
Or I could stretch out two fingers, yellowed with cold,
And stroke its black back,
But I know I would recoil.
And so earnestly I watch it,
A slow, calm, maternal gaze.
It twitches its beak in different directions
And, satisfied, disappears behind the bench
And out of sight.

PART IV

FULCRUM

69 *Regeneration*

So I survived and compromised with the mottled ground,
Which beckoned me hither and chased me thither,
And never let me be free.
But I lingered still.
Days come and go in drifting flow
And the straining after looking beyond,
Delving above and below,
Continuously in a mindless yawning cycle;
A still unfinished dress rehearsal,
Never to let me be free.
Sometimes I awake in dreams in deep, deep sleep
And see an excerpt of the real performance,
And then I sleep and love again
The old repetitions.

70 *Wakening*

Morning wakening,
The chalk-white air hanging adrift,
Empty the body and peaceful to float upon
No thought.
A line of waves pulls the body along in a horizontal,
Billow upon billow upon billow,
The pillow gapes in the middle
And the head sinks, the feet each weighed down
By a different rock
Begin to rise and float.
Eyes open to black and brown shapes and white spaces,
A dress thrown over a chair,
The sleeves droop,
Yellow and brown flowers with flecks of green.
Cannot identify these shapes.
Nothing matters.
The network of yesterday has disintegrated.
Chalk-white light. Rolling
Peace.

71 *Vision*

Stretched out in a darkened room
Opposite the orange dazzle of fire,
I wait for the headache to abate,
Tense network of nerves to loosen into coils
In the blackness behind the pink eyelid skin.
A craving to read,
It grows,
To read at full speed, to run headlong
Through a forest of sentences
And fill the restless mind with ideas.
A flicker of orange light,
Will not read, will not read,
Only to think slow thoughts, abstractions.
In the coal-black void I see the visual surface
Crumble away.
Pictures and colours and shapes no longer exist
Only to live, to live, to live,
Bouncing black coils unwind, unroll.
I open my eyes slowly
And as the colours steam into my soft eyes
I am reborn.

72 *The Losing*

I have forgotten it,
The guilt which lay on my back over the years
Like a woollen sack.
The peace that seizes me today
Is a cotton-wool gag
That muffles me and will not let me speak
The burden
Which I dare not remember.

73 *See-Saw*

Life is not symmetrical,
A layer of white icing upon the marzipan,
And a ring of angelica to complete the design.
For the wrongs, which I commit daily,
I cannot apologise,
Simply bear the see-saw rejoinder
Of wrongs heaped back on me,
And hope that somewhere between the two planks
Lies a fulcrum.

74 *Fulcrum*

If I could sink down into my stomach
And fall to rest upon a red velvet throne,
I would become my offspring and my master,
Silently to supervise day in, day out,
The child that feeds upon me.
No one knows where the centre lies:
Perhaps at this place, nodding to sleep
Upon the soft tufts of crimson,
Locked tightly within this black velvet cave,
Knowing only the dreadful waiting
For each moment to turn into the next:
Here lies the fulcrum.

75 *Keyboard*

There is a test-card C of selfhood,
Shades of happiness or worse.
Check the grey and black panels to find
The level at which you are really yourself,
And return to that key
As often as you dare,
So that you may spend
As much of your life as possible
At the correct pitch,
Day after day.

76 *Time Suspended*

Now that the pendulum has swung forward
To six o'clock summer,
Time lies suspended, spinning upon an axis
Of three o'clock,
Trapped in the middle of the office, where I sit,
Trapped in the shaft of sun upon the screw of my watch.
In this limbo anything can happen.
Far away the memory of winter,
The broken geyser in the bathroom,
And the lumps of ice and dirt-fleece
Upon the rim of the overnight glaze
On the bedside table.
Now that summer has melted us into the wallflowers,
Blazing blood-red on the windowsill,
We do not hurry or worry
Or think any more,
In this timeless wave of summer heat.
At this moment the grains of black markings
On the wooden desk
Gleam with polish and perspiration
Beneath my arm stretched out upon the wood.
Fragments of conversation
Spin around in a Catherine-wheel,
Spikes jutting out, overlapping at the edges,
Thoughts unfinished and unexplained
Will never be resolved, never, ever be explained.

THE DREAM OF STAIRS

A vacuum of time
That houses the breathing and the furniture of this room,
The shimmer of heat and trickle of sweat,
The sweat trickles, trickles down my arm,
Back into time,
Back through the needlepoint of light
On the screw of my watch
And the tips of the minute-hand.
A tick and a click
As the hands begin to move again,
Pulled back into the pool,
Magnetised to perform again
Their inescapable, unfinished drifting.

77 *Yoga Dance*

Yoga dance,
Fly away to the north and the south
Arms and legs gone I know not where,
Energy grows here.
I am one
With the ground below and all spaces;
There is evil in me.
I see it black as coal, a hard lump.
It glitters with silver spots.
Wrench it out
Of the spider cartwheel,
As I turn and flow,
There is emptiness here and aching –
Swallow it up.
The pink flesh will accept it whole
With curved palms
Pulling inwards
Dizzy cup of fear
Drink up the pain
And flow.

78 *The Vision*

Smile upon us, lazy beauty,
Out of custom, out of duty.
You need no hard-earned profession,
You exist on self-expression.
Smile with iridescent glow
On us poor, weary men below.

We have travelled far to find you.
Do our tired eyed remind you
Of yourself before your fame?
Though we moan, we do not blame
You for your leisurely existence
Just reward our long persistence.

Smile upon us, lazy beauty,
Out of custom, out of duty.
You need no hard-earned profession,
You exist on self-expression.
Smile with iridescent glow
On us poor, weary men below.

79 *Song of a Schizophrenic Monk*

What is the use of this strained sensibility
That aches and propels me towards infinity?
Mind-destructive, it yearns for an unfound sublimity
Ruinous to my remnants of sanity.
Sometimes momentarily relenting
I am released from this cruel dementing
Lingering longing for true affinity
With the one true symbol of deep-felt unity.

Weekdays pass in this odd community
Attitudes renewed and stances discarded,
A once fine intellect sadly retarded
By splitting trends in a crazed personality.

What is the use of this strained sensibility
That aches and propels me towards infinity?
Mind-destructive it yearns for an unfound sublimity
Ruinous to my remnants of sanity.

80 *The Singer*

Her voice hit the air with a subtle sweep,
Swallowed up the silence that had been,
Engulfed the fragments of physical existence
And the particles of air floating serene
And bound them together
Into one long, smooth bow of sound.

They listened satisfied as the old profound
Unanswered questions were resolved simple and straight.
No questions left to ask, though some still were
And all was understood like a long-standing joke.

Now the voice is changing, brittle, uneasy,
Communicating anguish, discontent,
And they are left so angry at this deceit
At losing one true moment, which had seemed complete.

81 *Heat*

Heat dissolves me, frees the barriers
Between my selfhood and the rest.
Cold makes me conscious of my tiny ego
In one small frame for ever compressed.
Heat expands me, melts me, frees me
To the fourth dimension, which never fails to please me.

Why do I wish to rejoin the world
From which I am parted by this body of bone?
My hands touch the chair, which rests by the table.
Once contact is reached, you are never alone.
The fire is wholesome and orange and good.
It warms my body and renews my selfhood.

The murmuring flames are cruel to the coal.
They eat it, devour it with torture refined.
One man's sorrow is another's reward
And coal is inferior breathing no mind.
So let heat expand me, meet me and free me
To the fourth dimension, which may yet redeem me.

82   *Nail Armour*

The torn fingernail, which you will pull off
In spite of itself
Grappled with its parent-body and will not be removed.
Magnetic loyalty,
Conventional adherence.
Cannot live and grow outside the flesh-roots,
So hangs on,
Vestigial organ of a former animal.
Man had once a coat of nail
Before God changed it
Into a sheath of skin,
Regrets its melting
And will go back to the old brittle armour of pearl.

83 *The Waiting*

The black days,
Metallic white sky clinking upon stone pavements,
When no thoughts arise;
Only a waiting in the head
For a hand to pull you out of the vacuum
Into the foam of bubble-movement.
Primitive variety of colours,
Fragile skins
That will burst surely.
An illusion, that softens the knife-edge
Between the merging of sky and stone
And prevents pulsating explosion.

No-one here,
Not a soul,
No-one here.
The monk in his cell,
Weeds creeping inside the grey stone,
Could not be more alone
Than this furnace of waiting.
Long ago, when the dinosaur stepped out,
Wriggled over the boulders,

THE DREAM OF STAIRS

There was air and white sky.
When the molecule rolled away
From the atoms all around,
It charged into a new area of space.
Now the streets are crowded
With the light of sun and moon.
People are lollipops along the pavements
And shops that dazzle,
A thousand theatres, new facades,
Old paint flaking away from hooded eyes
In gallery frames,
Watchful,
Derived from the electrical skulls
Buried long ago in Florence and The Hague.
They tell of a journey that must be taken,
A long tightrope through time and space,
Along with the dinosaurs,
And the weeds twining into the crevices of the abbey,
That will not let go, never let go their cling,
Growing thicker, stronger,
While inside the monk waits alone,
Here he is alone
In a furnace of silence and grey stone.

In the tube
Light hangs from bare bulbs and black squares
Reflecting my face alone in the window;
Outside
The tunnels scream into a game of running.
Here the long upholstered benches lie in wait,
A no-man's land,
Empty as waiting rooms,
That lead in dreams to strange halls crowded with faces,
Smiling, grinning.
Here there are only vertical lines upon the planked floor,
Lines that are lines
And nothing more
And never will be,
Grey with screws of steel that gleam like stars
To bear away the eyes.

This hour is every hour,
Waiting for what can
Never come to pass.
The concrete and glass outside bring no comfort,
Nor the sweep of bird-flutter across in a diagonal.
Slowly
The sun burns an electric star
On top of the rood opposite
Against the white metal of sky.

84 *Lizard*

In another life
Many transmigrations ago
I was a lizard.
Unthinking wriggling indolence
Among the Palaeolithic ferns
And rivers of ooze,
To squelch in whatever direction whim chose,
To stretch out, coils extended over the damp grass
And think a blue sky.
This strange change
Not easy to live a human,
Schematic thought unnatural.
Want to return to my old horny skin
And cast off this soft, pink flesh.

85 *Feathers*

Today,
Floating on an eiderdown of sunshine,
Feathers drifting out, softly twirling,
I smile at the sun-shadows, curled up in my chair.
Across the room the girl on the telephone
Makes plans for an abortion
With cool practicality,
Bony fingers wired against the telephone chords,
Shrill voice echoes the tinkle,
As she puts the receive down.
If only I could share it, her shock, her plans, her fear,
Bottled up like the body inside her.
The surgeon will pare the foetus away with a knife,
And the embryo will disappear,
And the more I unwind into sleepy indolence,
The more she stiffens to protect the unborn child
From dismemberment.

86 *Nightmare*

To wake up from a three o'clock nightmare
Of a Black Mass –
Two men cross-legged
In front of steaming bowls of liquid,
Chanting smoke and shadows,
In a huge oak-beamed hall;
People drifting slowly towards the door,
Manipulated by some devilish charm;
To wake up in the brain-ticking silence
Of the box bedroom,
Unbreathable black air,
Old thoughts rolling over and over,
Until the heaviness begins to evaporate
Into the release of dawn.

87 *The Bag*

Bought on an impulse,
It cost three days of summer dust
And weighed down
With the bulk of cream and red leather.
The shopkeeper had reduced the price by half,
Fatigued by the woman's rusted face,
As she wavered in the shadows of the shop,
The alcoves of the afternoon heat.
Out of doors
The handles clung softly,
Sickening as coach upholstery,
Impregnated with petrol fumes,
That bounce along hygienic journeys
In the dazzle of sky and field and open road.
Soon she knew the bag would be discarded
Along with sentences spoken out of turn
And thoughts
Too turbulent to bear recollection.

88 *The Open Door*

Cannot live glad hours all the time,
Red cushions and sparkling wine.
Must know the throb of the no-way-out,
The surprise of old deeds turned sour.
Cannot breathe the fresh air every day,
Must gulp at open train doors, wind rushing by;
And the eye-smarting grit a reminder of
Old atoms falling away and turning enemy.

89 *Illusion*

You would like me better
If the grey ghost of sadness flickered around my face,
Binding me to you with my need,
A transparent gauze.
Instead I feel the cut of happiness,
That wells up irrepressibly every day
With the green leaves, the wallflowers
And the jostle of the crowds.
I cannot deny my exuberance:
The morning jokes, the lazy afternoon.
But sometimes in the evenings at nine o'clock or so,
When the bubbles of day have simmered away,
The grey ghost of sadness flickers round my face,
And I belong to you.

90 *Nocturne*

Midnight in my square bedsitter
With the electric fire aflame,
An orange iced-lolly frozen into heat,
The splutter of hidden water within the geyser,
A pop song next door splintered
Into three sounds by a faulty needle.
I should be asleep, cut off from the squeal of the night,
But the black sky outside is a friend
Whom I cannot bear to leave.
Wakefulness is a luxury,
When there is no need for action.
I will make my life as useful as the dented kettle,
Silver-grey upon the tiny stove.
The fire scorches, the gas ring hisses,
But the geyser is silent
And I wait for a sign that this craving
Curved arrow of the heart
Will be acknowledged.

91 *Poetry*

To run into a long tunnel, blackness, cannot breathe
And write the subconscious helter-skelter out
Into the blue-green sky-trees open air,
A world of white tablecloths, pass the salt please
And live for a patch of non-think refreshment,
Until the ticking mounts to an alarm-clock signal,
Time once again to dive into the tunnel,
Behind pink eyelids let the brain-thoughts pour over
Into words.

92 *Skull-Light*

The God in my head is more real
Than the traffic-lights' winking rubies
On a Sunday morning.
They will be wiped off that face
A starlight's throw from now.
While the God in my head
Will go ticking on
In the molten lava
Of the grinning earth
For ever.

93 *Selfhood*

There is no cure for being one person
And not two or three,
No way to puncture the skin
And let the self out and the air in,
No quick route to becoming an atom in the universe.
Each day the words fly to and fro,
Linking together two bodies of brain.
The grey cells crinkle with thoughts blended.
There is no way to evade
The silent shine of the sun on the pavements
Clinking beneath your heels,
As you move through the air
Locked in a bottle of skin.

I slip away from his magnetic force every day,
Shaken up by fragments of colour and telephone calls.
If only I could stay
Locked within the black shape of fear,
The fear of Him, that makes me tremble
And shake back into humility,
Away from the fluorescent lights
And the gimmicks of leisure
Into the cold rock-being of selfhood.

94 *Spider*

You are a spider flashing out silks,
A crochet network of your whims and fancies
A symmetrical design praised by many,
And often displayed in exhibitions.
Yet I see in the crossings of thread
A multitude of tiny flies caught and squashed
To reinforce the joints of the meshwork
With their dead bodies.

95 *Interval*

Sleep in wonder.
Do not know where the soul goes;
Hushed to its Father
Or under the earth,
Evil, washed out in the shadows of the window-sill,
Bleached into the white dawn,
Falling like salt
In streaks
Around the drifting bedroom;
Trembles
Between the leaping colours of morning
And in the momentary death,
Hanging,
The balance is steady.
Weighted down with all the love
That wings around the room.
Strange eyes in dreams,
Black as Lethe,
Call you back.

PART V

SHELL

96 *Shell*

I am a shell
Catching echoes of the past
And pearl-flashes of the future.
Satisfaction pervades me in an iridescent glow.
Yet I am brittle and low.
I have withstood the flow of the years
With my strange protective exterior,
But I am flimsy and insecure:
A kick will send me flying down the beach
Into the beckoning sea
And I will return thinner and more battered than before.
For I am insecure
And my beauty is lent by the flickering sunlight
And the swirling whorls of my interior.
The sea to me superior
Whispers and gurgles in its immensity,
But I do not wish to be crusted into pulp
And to merge with the drifting sand beneath the sea.
No. I wish to be free and whole and me.

97 *Love*

My heart like frozen seaweed hangs suspended
Upon the iceberg of the silent river,
Until a wave of love arrives to free it
From the newly melted tentacles for ever.

It spreads its flattened form upon the ripples
Of the water bubbling chill on the hidden ice,
Content with the slow resolving of its motion,
Retarded by the snow on the water's face.

When suddenly a breeze arrives to pull it
Far away from the frozen depths of that location:
It flutters into movement swimming smoothly,
Now active after years of cold stagnation.

98 *Creation*

Two decades and a half have passed,
The spider's silk is spinning fast.
And you bear a child in your silent womb,
Your child needs care, mine understanding.
Two decades and a half have passed,
The spider's silk is spinning fast.

Many years have flashed since vacuum,
Many years to tick till judgement,
Still the problem needs resolving,
Yours needs care, mine understanding.
Two decades and a half have passed,
The spider's silk is spinning fast.

99 *Fear*

No one
Can wipe out the fear that is within you.
Though you collect around you a large circle of friends
To lean upon, each with a different handle,
Still the points of light make you blink in fright,
The silver rings flash against your vision,
Swirling dizziness.
Nothing
Can assuage your unrest,
Though you block out the overhanging shadows,
The clash of colour.
With each obstacle overcome
A new enemy appears on the horizon,
The farther out to sea you travel.
Only accept this black unrest,
Breathe deeply, rocking with the waves,
Grey tongues lashing,
And be discomforted.

100 *Conviction*

I lay on the garden hammock
Stared up at the sky
And tried to pretend that there was no God.
And all over the city people were leading separate lives,
Unlinked and to no purpose.
I chopped the population into pieces with a wire grill
And saw a fragmented swarm;
But as I stared back at the sky,
Soft cotton wool frozen into infinite benevolence,
I was not convinced,
And slowly the wire-grill disappeared
And the people were joined together again
Into a compound of love.

101 *Being*

Fallen away
From the old God-love-bond,
Black iron bar magnet,
Splinter in my heart,
That pricks and makes it tick.
Today,
Free as blue clouds,
I see the space of breathing
And wonder
Where is the core.

102 *Energy*

Every day
Springs forth twins
From the womb kaleidoscope.
Leaves form chains.
We are all one and growing.
The sap
Juice twines between poles apart.
If one day
Can coil two rows of words,
What will the next day bring?
Who will emerge and who will be lost,
Scowled aside
By a downward wish
Of the will turned awry.
In that moment of choosing,
Flicker to the left or right,
Whether to take the stretching outwards
Reach towards some light
Through the funnel
Yellow flicker;
In that moment of choosing,
The day grows twins,
Amoeba divides,
Impulse of outreach.
We are all one and growing.

103 *Pulse*

Stay attuned to the forces of life,
Revolving wheel hub circle,
Merry-go-round and spin daily.
Feel here the slow rub grind
Of falling leaves, that endless flow
Will not let go,
Magnet to hold blue-back
The streak of sky,
Where silent lies,
That used to grow,
Crushed by the flow,
That wants to be let out,
Go, go,
Stay attuned to the flow
And grow
To be saved
From the green-edged teeth of flame,
Where dragons grin in hellfire
Pain,
To resolve the washed days,
That slipped into the drain, the flow,
Long ago, spotlight hours,
That live on in remembered shame
And grow.

104 *Continue*

Pass on to the next.
It grows.
Dandelion clock puffs spiders;
Cornflower swirls
Will be a new figure on tomorrow's mirror.
Cannot believe the looking-glass retina
That sees
Each new two eyes upon a nose
Differently the next hour
From any other.
Words scatter four hours from now.
In this evening's café
Alphabet noodles in the soup
Chew into different reproaches
Around the linen table.
Why cannot they be all one friendly chewing soul?
Instead,
Split into fenced people,
Acids
Blow up the pasta
Into flesh.
Do not know,
Cannot believe and yet should know,
That on tomorrow's mirror
A new figure will appear.
Pass on to the next.

105 *Puppet*

I am a puppet,
Jerking one and two and three and four
In time to the command.
My wooden cheeks gleam in the daylight
And I weep hygienic tears,
Because I want to be loved by everyone,
Not just one or two or three,
But every puppet that jerks beneath the sun.
They creak through this robot world,
Teeth clacking, arms cracking and feet snapping,
In time to the daily performance.
I cry hygienic tears with my varnished eyes,
Because there is only one other puppet,
Who with his fist-cracking skill, can pull the strings
To release me from this stiff rhythm
Into a graceful dance.
And so each time I clatter through the crowds
And barricades of wooden figures,
I long for a glimpse of the strange puppet-man,
Who alone can turn me into flesh and blood.

106 *Nature*

Nature often belies living experience
And living experience is often belied by time.
What comes is felt. It passes and dissolves
Into a fragment as tiny as this rhyme.
A mass of wadding lies between the grains
Of living matter, which alone endure.
These minute sparks elude my searching hand
And drift away according to their law.
I try in vain to grasp at entity,
But when I trap an atom it explodes.
Destruction snatches up my outstretched arm
And I know all too well what death forebodes.
Oh let me be content with what is here
In its familiar state, nor try to pierce
The smoke of gloom which delicately veils
The form of entity alive and fierce.

107 *Ago*

The broken-down fire
Fuses the flat at dawn
Into an older winter.
Red flares across the snow,
As the moon treads heavily.
Soon the wolves will sing and howl,
The curves of ice will sweep across the earth,
The hulk of sky and mountaintops
Will spin into sleep.
No-one cares.
Alone
The bodies in caves
Wait for the whining to abate
And roast back into black comfort,
Breathing like metronomes
To balance
The terror
Out there.

108 *Tunnel*

One soul was lost.
It went tumbling down the hill,
A green hoop,
Stalk-tender shining on the bend
Of light,
Ringing in the air
Basel and garlic and thyme.
It lay curved in the stomach of a child
And slipped over the edge of the square world
Before Galileo demolished it.
I will swim through fire,
Orange and gold, peeling
Into blood
And out of humanity
To find again
After the long coffin-race
Eyes burnished with
Understanding.

109 *Maternity*

On this afternoon,
Tranquil gold,
I would like to have children.
I feel a swelling and a ruffle of feathers.
I will protect,
Teach them my hard-won peace,
Unravelling year by year the secret of flight.
Yellow layers of four o'clock.
All over London mothers are wiping
Grey soap-suds off red fingers.
They pause and listen to the silence of sleeping children.
I, too, share the unknown with the unknowing,
Who have not yet come to birth,
But lie sleeping in beds of yellow seed
Within my womb.

110 *No Mother*

Fear of motherhood.
A broken glass does not matter,
Can be replaced by our own goodwill,
But not the soft fontanelle and the incessant cry.
Unknown cause of complaint.
Total dependence, desire for explanation
Of its own discomfort,
Reassurance that, in fact, there is no need to wail.
Cushioned reconciliation.
This I cannot give
Knowing not myself.
I see the world through a magnifying glass,
Each pore of conflict multiplied by ten.
My future baby is to me the macrocosm.
I cannot console it.

111 *Development*

Baby breathing, mother peeping
Doctor smiling, baby sleeping,
Noise and peace in rhythmic flow
Form that human embryo.

Stories, music, liquid, babbling,
Laughter, clapping anger, squabbling
Noise and peace in rhythmic flow
Form that human embryo.

When he reaches adult status
Makes that sudden, cruel hiatus,
Leaving simple childhood dream life,
Pushing, striving, marrying dream wife.

Age comes slowly, dropping sweetly,
Contemplates his death maturely,
Noise and peace in rhythmic flow
Shapes that immortal embryo.

112 *Release*

The girl in purple trousers lay on the carpet,
Pressed down against the ground,
Willing herself away from the encounter group,
Shut her eyes into blackness.
A hand prodding her in the ribs
Broke through the barrier,
A gasp and then a strangulated cry,
As the coal-fire of tears broke through the black air,
Down, down, down into the past,
The flames flicker against the black coals,
The flames of the love she felt
And the blackness of his silence.
The waves of sobbing scream out,
Body sinking deeper into the hard floor,
Falling into the past,
Until all the blackness is expelled
And there is only weeping.

113 *The Talents*

To pay back in energy
The gift I have been given:
Upon the kitchen table seven chocolate pennies
Wrapped in gold
And a chocolate sixpence.
My daughter fiddles with the first,
Methodically unwraps the gold skin,
A slither of silver curls up from underneath.
She eats with upturned eyes, her face is solemn.
I see that each chocolate is a decade,
And I have only four more pennies to go and a sixpence,
To reach my span.
She plays with the pennies.
Endless possibilities for her.
I put them in a row.
My one goal
In recompense of natural egotism,
I will repay with work upon work upon work,
No limits to my labour,
Until I have consumed myself,
Melted away the last drippings of chocolate.

114 *Decision*

Where the will lies
Flicker to the right and the left
The candle might blink
Out of the tunnel
An eye
Open sight
Distinguishes volition,
Goes this way,
Turns back
But does not know the impetus.
In recollecting loses;
Will be one again
When oblique
It stumbles
Through
Shutters.

He made a decision at that point of time,
Feet dabbling in the sunlight squares,
Reflection of the open window,
To refer all moments and decisions
To the will of God,
To lasso all future experience,
Rope after rope,
Coil after coil
Catching a retreating figure here
And there a falling tree-trunk,
Before the act is completed.
Strange free-will
For is it so?
He will never know
Whether this moment of choice
Was his choosing
Or predetermined,
Before his brain began to spin.

PART VI

WATER

115 *Twentieth Century*

I am a child of the twentieth century;
I have found no hammock to hide in,
No cause to separate me from these unsettled times,
And as the century fragments,
So do I split, ebb and flow.

I am become the twentieth century
And if I live to be old, old,
So will the century flood over
Into the twenty-first
And we will trickle away together.

116 *Individuation*

I hear an inner thump and must express
The useless Weltschmerz and the emptiness,
The flow of a million minds, where thought and void
In alternating patterns weave and blend
A melody of insight and distress,
Confusing to all human speculation,
Unanswerable to close investigation.
Only the powers above can sift and mend
The whirled confusion of that deep recess,
And only the strength of truth can heal and bless
The strange divergent ways to which we trend,
And to God Himself will I confirm
When I finally reach my destined end.

117 Tryptich

To hear sometimes the grey groan of the Cross,
Sometimes the whisper that no redemption is possible,
To hear sometimes the weeping of the six million,
Sometimes the whisper that their suffering was in vain;
These are the whispers I hear on either side
As the coach shoots along the dusty avenues of trees
In the flickering morning sunlight.
Birches, oaks and willows
Crackle against the window-panes in loops and tangles
And I foresee a world
Crazily overgrown by trees and people,
Where what is believed is often untrue,
And what is untrue is often successful.

118 *Question*

The Man on the Cross, He rose,
Who knows whether this is true?
For no-one alive has the Methuselah memory
To look back and weep in recall.
But I see every day
A man from his pinnacle of pain
Stretch out to reach God and come to life again,
Mysterious conversion.
And so I believe sometimes,
And sometimes I do not believe,
And in my doubt I find a pinnacle so high
That I think I can never reach the top
And be reborn again.

THE DREAM OF STAIRS

Was Jesus sad,
When He hung with sad eyes exalting,
Black wells of knowing
And reached out through the thin air to the voice above,
Or was it the voice in His head?
Was He mad,
When He soothed centuries of half-people with promises,
And gave them placebos of a black-tunnel world to come?
Am I false
If I drift into the blue particles of sunlit water,
Salt sand yellow ripples,
And through the clusters of pearl-blue-veined shells
I see in the glints of silver,
That He is there?
Was He mad, selfless mistake unending,
And am I false
In my obstinate wishing?

119 *Devils*

When I was fifteen,
I stood in front of a painting by Breughel,
The lid of Hell and a thousand seething demons,
Thick red splashes of paint mingled with lurid greens.
Today I see beneath your smiling face a thousand hatreds,
And behind the cupboard in the attic,
The flesh of a dead rat is mouldering away
Into sticky decay,
And I am too busy to keep track
Of my devilled thoughts, as they wriggle by,
Or to incite the demons that are dehydrated
And polished back into respectability.

120 *Duel*

Twin pawns of ivory on a chessboard,
Good and evil, black and white;
And when after a complex strategy.
Brain move upon brain move,
Good wins.
The battle is still waiting for the next game.

121 *Twins*

She laughed. 'I looked out of the window just now
And saw two girls in yellow shirts.
They both patted their hair at the same time.'
Her mouth opened into a black slit,
Eyes rolling from right to left,
Trying to grasp it;
Brown pupils like marbles
Seeking to crash against the giant ball,
And bouncing back in vain.
I looked through the sunlit window,
Trying to locate the yellow shirts,
But saw instead my face reflected back,
Black slit mouth, eyes rolling,
And wondered whether the two girls
Had been watching us.

122 *Spur*

I have nothing,
Unless I have all.
The perpetual falling short
Pinches me harder and harder,
Until I have reached as far as I can go,
Almost a peace of wry resignation,
That soon dwindles into a fraction of what I seek.

123 *Holocaust*

'There is an answer to every problem,
If you look hard enough,'
Said the blond boy, thin lips glistening behind gold beard.
But I see so many people rubbing together unhappily,
The patterns that go awry and cannot be endured
Except by evasion.
Perhaps in times of danger he always rushes
To the nearest fire-escape
And never looks back to stare
At the burning blood-pools and screaming bodies,
Face to face.

124 *Conflict*

The soul searcher
Lays aside his pen
And watches the plastic mosaic on the restaurant table,
Blue leaves and orange bells
Against a background of yellow;
The artist's aim
To fit the colours into the right shapes
And draw the eyes into a pattern of contentment,
That leaves no room for speculation.
If only he could exchange his see-saw stance
Of right and wrong
For the skill of a finished visual product,
Which knows that final flash of aesthetic relief,
Denied to him by his refusal to rest at any conclusion.

125 *Reclamation*

Wish to be reclaimed by the Spirit
Now that I am unravelled by doubts.
Want to be resolved into certainty,
Now that my eyes splay to the left and right,
Will cling to the wish.
Will wish a stronger want.
My want I recognise as a need.
But valid none the less.
The gap in me
A vestigial organ withered, which was once
A healthy limb.

126 *Doubt*

They are mocking the devils within me,
The little gold gods that sit upon high in judgement.
They have seen the mouldering fungus beneath my shell.
If I could recover the old gold of solid rock,
And laugh at the sun,
I would do so willingly.
But I am bound to the rock of selfhood
And must grin and bear the mumble and nidge
Of the mocking black spirits within me.
They gnaw away at my entrails,
Not all the day long, by no means,
But sometimes in the butterlight of midday,
When I would wish to share the peaceful glow
Of the little gold gods upon high,
They probe and niggle.

127 *Panorama*

A swarm of birds fly fanlike overhead
And I cannot keep track of them.
Endless directions. Weltschmerz.
In a flash of memory
I see a woman ironing shirts
In a kibbutz laundry-hut.
The steel heat sweeps to and fro
Creating a new crease to blot out the old,
And no one watches.
Damp air rises over the white cloth.
Fresh cotton threads between the yellowing buttons.
Through the windows above, a Wedgwood sky
Burns down onto a crescent of avocado trees
And no-one counts the number.

128 *Corrupt*

I am a turnip gone mouldy
And my top is falling off.
I am vinegar turned sour
And I am valued now more highly
Than before as sparkling wine,
But I know that I am lost.
I am a fungus, rare delicacy,
And I would like to find again
The old molecular groupings
That strung me together long ago
And go back, back.

129 *Black Star*

Black star
Make me strong
Against the pale of night.
Hide from me no yawning caves
In this moment of time beyond the clock
Nothing shall be draped aside
To save the soul from shock,
For the white stars have turned black,
And the moon is hidden
By my knowing what lies beyond the shine
Of nocturnal quiet.
The shadows have cracked away
And the clouds gape open
To show
The dizzy pulling towards some other star,
That cannot be seen,
Black star
That may seem evil
Because it brings the terror
Of screaming darkness,
Expose her hidden places
And shine upon all that is truthful,
The prick
Of being.

130 *Awakening*

The day I put away the tranquillisers
I awoke to a scream of colour, sharp-edged cars
Racing down the road
And tiny printed letters
Jumping out at me from newspapers.
A band of steel cut into my forehead, clanging adrenalin
Running riot inside my brain,
As I walked over the classic pavement
With jerky stops, surprised at the rolling air,
The stone of the ground.
People flitted past as lightly on all sides,
And I could not help smiling without my happy pills.

131 *Water*

Thirst.
A crystal glass ball of ice-cold water,
Salt pain, salt thirst, salt parching salt.
To sway blood pounding in the temples, hot and cold.
If only cold water, iced water, melted icebergs,
Pouring down in rivulets into long-tunnelled glasses,
Crystal facets, rainbow streaked.
Rainbows caught and frozen and melted
Into long, long gulps, long gulps of icy water.
If the desert sun beat down, sand all around,
Dune stretches on all sides, far, far away on all sides
And no hope of water,
How could I bear it?
The soldier in the battlefield, alone,
Hidden between the trenches,
Would like to drink once more,
But fears that cold water will never come, never,
No water, never, no crystal transparency,
Only the opaque streaks of mud, brown and sticky,
Lingering.

THE DREAM OF STAIRS

The Man on the Cross knew that water would not come.
He gasped and grasped it. He accepted it.
The poet, when thoughts are scarce,
Shrivels up. He fears that ideas will never come, never.
A drought, a parching thirst, a vacuum.
Thirst.
A crystal glass ball of iced-cold water.
Salt pain, salt thirst, salt parching salt.
Perhaps cold water, iced water will never come,
No, will never come,
Never.

132 *Weep Before God, Laugh Before Men*

Weep before God
When the ice breaks through, snaps brittle surface of crust
And the black chill of water
Underneath bubbles into fiery heat,
When into the driftwards of the underworld
You are sucked,
Never to know the answer,
And laugh before men,
Golden hearts swollen to love-burst,
For the brown sinews are friendly
And grip you into peace,
When the old jokes of long acquaintance pull you back
Into the magnetic field.
Weep before God, when the blackness in your heart
Drags you into the terror of endless floating,
The Hell of listening to the brain-tick
Each moment growing large
As it rises to fall into the next beat of time
And laugh before men,
As they multiply day by day,
Searching and loving, pins on the tiny point of a magnet,
Floating around the vacuum of this huge constellation.

133 *Suicide*

A glass of water and a tube of monotonous pills.
Pearls of death to kill you,
But not to resolve your problems.
These linger on annoyingly after your body has died
And the mortals who remain in compromising life
Must resolve these as well as attend to
Your dreary funeral.

A buzzing in your ears and a palpitating heart.
Unconsciousness is near.
Lingering death is not for you nor pain, you hope.
But to take the easy way out
You weaken in drugged oblivion and die.
You coward
And fool.
Yet deserving of much compassion and understanding.

I fear not death,
For it sifts life's soggy bread and milk
Into curds and whey.
My dead self will attain either nothingness
Or complete unity with the universe,
And then I will be at peace.

It is life's ambiguity,
Shadow upon meaningless shadow,
Which I hate and dread.
The hostile face, the twisted accusing finger,
The love ignored or ridiculed,
Too quickly fed,
The relentless complexity of new day and new tomorrow.

Therefore weak, but resolute,
He jumped into the black river,
Purged of momentary hesitation by the scorching
Ice ripples,
And choking bitter waters.

134 *Silence*

White dots in the air
That fizzle
And want to speak.
The silence pounds noisily against my ears.
I hear the wheeze of breathing,
Crackling hair, soft swish of sleeves against the chair.
I stand poised, a stone within a catapult,
About to be hurled into speech;
Pulled back
As the master hand of reticence presses me down
Into thundering silence.

PART VII

THE NINGO PIN

135 *Chawton House*

In Chawton House, the birthplace of Jane Austen,
Regency symmetry, peace and elegance intermingle,
White walls, a ballroom dress, a hanging tapestry,
A creaking door 'purposely left, so that Jane
Should have warning of approaching visitors.
And could put away the manuscript in hand'.
Why so?
When today the manuscript is the only part of her
That has survived?
Her inner life revealed to the queuing public
Could not be disclosed
To the passing relatives outside her door;
Or perhaps the intrusion
Would have jolted her back into reality
Away from her tasteful moulding, transformation
Of the muffled scenes behind the creaking door.

136 *She Searched for Happiness*

She searched for happiness
As if it were her right.
The right of a woman
To live and to be.

She searched for happiness
Wishing for the right.
The right of women
To enjoy and luxuriate.

She searched for happiness
Which was her right.
But needless to say
She did not find it.

137 *Alien*

You, who dwell in a cold and Nordic region,
A stagnant place, where nothing is forgiven,
Release me from my pity and my sorrow
And come back home. We'll bear you no derision.
Nothing is mocked at here; no one will stare,
I hate to think you'll wither and age out there.

We know you and we love you
While you stayed here,
We asked no questions, probed you with no glances,
Be what you will. Come home, all is forgiven
And make this life a pleasant bridge to Heaven
For now you ache and suffer far away,
Loathing yourself in meaningless dismay.

The day you went away my heart was shattered.
It crumbled into many prickling pieces,
Each time I think of you I weep and shudder
And my regret renews and still increases.
Nothing is mocked at here; no one will stare.
I hate to think you'll wither and age out there.

138 *Afterwards*

Is this an eternal waking,
After the eye has shut onto death,
Waiting for what can
Never come to pass;
No ear to hear diversion,
No wrist to stretch out to another?

Now
The blank screen remembers
The whole face
Of the past.
Primeval and cave black
It reflects back to the present,
Like two mirrors astride opposite walls
Dwindled into silver shadows.

Now the whole
Tumultuous course of events.
That formed one life
Must be unravelled
Before it can find peace.

139 *Shock*

This death
I cannot quite believe in.
Cannot believe in at all.
She will come walking into the room tomorrow
Surely,
Face crumpled pin with laughter,
Arms swaying sideways,
Brisk clump of footsteps,
Cannot believe that in silence she lies
In a wooden box, hidden ground-deep
And I will never see her again,
Ever.

140 *To Grieve*

Cannot feel a proper sorrow,
Cannot reach back to the black source of being
That will whisper the words of grief to me for
This death so sudden.
Only surprise and a twinge of remorse
For my numbness,
As though this had lopped off the tall stem,
Chopped into two stalks
A life that was reaching out, growing.
Now at last the black waves
Curve upwards and roll over me,
And I grieve for the person that lived,
And for the second person that will never be,
Perhaps somewhere,
Condensed in blackness,
But never unravelled with the slow white life-years.

141 *Grief*

On the corner of the arcade
Between the mahogany display
And the vases of spring flowers,
A woman in suede is fierce with tears.
Her face has cracked into triangles and points,
And the brown leathery skin, once smart,
Is now shiny and sodden.
Her jaunt habit of walking still remains
To mock her heavy shoulders and neck craned forwards,
Hiding the twisted shock,
And I alone at this split second of time
Know that she has lost someone, something,
Black gloves crumpled into the palm of her hand,
Something that can never again be recovered.

142 Roses

At three o'clock
The line that cuts the afternoon in two,
The roses begin to fall.
They have fallen every year of my life.
I see them fall in the garden of four-years old
Fall beneath the blackening storm-sky,
When the rain tumbled down onto a white silk handbag.
They fall outside the long windows
Of the college dining-hall
Fall in sunlight patterns, that fix
The silent girls frozen over their motionless hands
For ever,
Strange silver sunlight that makes them sombre.
And now they fall, pink scattering saucers,
Onto a figure walking down the path.
I may never see him again,
Perhaps once or twice,
But never as before,
When the sweep of bush-roses fluttered down
Pulling us away with their coral scent,
Away to the original source,
Where there was no scattering of showerburst,
But only the compressed ball of clutched flowers,
As they once grew in the beginning
Before the Fall.

143 *Return*

I felt myself falling through a hole in the ground,
Down, down into the gloom,
The terror of dizzy dropping,
Sick lurching of the heart,
As the white hole at the top
Grows further and further away
And the hope of reaching light again
Diminishes.
Trapped in the gloom with my empty mind
I reach at last the soft earth at the bottom
To confront myself face to face,
The gloom at the base of my being
And sink with relief into the springy soil
Able to breathe again.

It came back to me,
After days of waiting,
Surged slowly back to touch the cliffs,
And I was filled once more
With the knowing.
Long minutes of spiky-edged waiting
Pressed into concertina flat folds of time-doubt,
Compared with the moments of
      hours of
      days of
Feeling Him there.

144   *I Wonder What This Constellation Will Be*

I wonder what this constellation will be
Five eras from now?
Will my vibrations still be roaming
Around the black sky
Along with a myriad of others,
Notes in a gigantic silent symphony,
And my bones fossilised into chemical components
Of the earth?
Will there be anywhere – a spot, a shadow –
Which I can call me?
My thoughts to live on in the dreams
Of clairvoyant sleepers
To flash through the nightly hum
Of all that has ever been?
And will my words be remembered by some God,
Who, if He exists, will think from time to time
Of one idiosyncratic specimen
Who flowed out of His creative release
Black speck among an endless torrent of spawn?

145 *Forwards*

Each one of us
Will one day be broken,
Spirit wrenched aside
As years ago the ship's surgeon
Would saw at wasted limbs,
Hiss of the flesh
Falling away beneath his knife
That could never keep rhythm with the burning shrieks.
One day
When some of the mystery has departed,
Yet still a release of surprise
At the actual moment –
What will happen?

146 *Resurgence*

The empty spaces and wasted days,
Hours frozen by love grown old and decayed,
And minutes paralysed by dust,
Where do they lie, these spaces and places?
Between the grimy cracks of the pavement
That grate and twist, as we tread them down darkly,
Or are they grounded deep into the earth
And crushed back into our bodies,
Lying afloat,
To re-emerge in the seeds of future children
That live out old negative moments
And perform strange, unpredictable deeds?

147 *Gold Door*

There is a gold door in the sky;
However hard I knock
It will not open,
Never open.
Brown cloud told me so.
No it will never open until death
Slowly to reveal the gaping crack.
If I could be content
To tingle with probing knuckles,
Never to crack the surface crust,
Nor scratch the fibres with pins.
On good days,
Slow blow of wind tapping,
I hear soft voices
All around
And feel the yellow metal
Glide beneath my silent palms.

148 *When the Door Opens*

When the door opens
The silence will be broken
The finger-bones of air will filigree to ivory.
Meanwhile the gramophone of memory
Plays out old scenes
Recalled
In waiting;
When the door opens
The speckled lace of air will tear to shreds.
The streets outside wink rubies
Fluorescent over shop façades,
Heels clink like water in a well
And echoes fall away.
If the door will never open,
The room square and frozen
Will be a blind coffin
And play out old gramophone records forever.

INDEX OF FIRST LINES

149 *Save This Soul*

Save this soul
Catch its dropping
Through the net before it peters away.
Freeze it, consolidate it,
Hold it fast within the iron will
Forever.

150 *The Ningo Pin*

I'll give you a ningo pin,
A pin of God,
A tiny pinnacle of ice,
Minute and scarcely visible,
One end a bulk, a minute swelling,
The other a crystal, pricking point,
A slither of frozen water –
A ningo pin.

It will bring you luck
Wherever you may dwell,
A glowing flicker of superstition
To glitter and twinkle forever,
An echo of the happiness you have known
And all that is yet to come.

One hot summer day
When the scorching sun
Breathes fire on the torrid ground
My pin will melt and trickle away,
A droplet of nullity,
A frozen zero,
A mere shadow of a pin.

151 *Inconsolation*

The death of someone you love,
Unknown agony,
Cannot be consoled,
It is the death of God
And the mystery in them
Will never be discovered.

152 *The Soul*

The human soul floats down from Heaven,
At the dawn of the day of the life's long span
And up again it will later return
To rest in the place where it first began.
Existence is one long procession
Of alternations in human succession.
The actions remain, but the players are new,
A million permutations link
The thoughts of a hundred decades ago
With what today you are tempted to think
In one long unending ebb and flow.
The soul, which rises, must afterwards sink
And the only fact we certainly know
Is that all is resolved as death's circular brink.

153 *Waves*

The waves roll in
Day after day
And beyond the ocean
People grow old.
Grey lace of water,
Fringe of brown lace
Grows old beneath the clinking teacups,
China white as the bones of a skull,
Burnt dry as ivory in the rays of the sun,
Cleaned by salt and pared away,
Bones change to fossils and people decay,
Day after day;
Continual switch from the rocks to the shore,
As the sea edges the cliffs away from the sand,
Burnt away by the pressure of water,
Slowly the cities move and change,
Like snakes coiling up as the years roll by,
The phrases change and alternate
And people move to another land,
Grey lace of water,
Fringe of brown lace
And the waves roll in.

154 *Insight*

The spirit entered them;
Salt smoking a tumbler of water
Could not cloud so much.
Ectoplasm
Against the attic door
Could never creak so much
As their surprised bones
When the spirit entered.
It was not peace;
The frozen evening
Tongued
Their hands into pink leather,
Clenched thumbs and fingers into silken sausages
To keep away the pain.
It was not perception.
The street they walked along was
Heavy,
Cast a gate of shadow.
There was sick surprise
Beneath the glassy wind.
When the spirit entered
There was hesitation.

Hanging cheeks, weigh down with the ache of ideas,
That can never be resolved.
No juxtaposition can bring to balance
The scales that hang awry,
Weighted down
By a curiosity, that is infinite.
Only when by chance
In a pure moment
A vision emerges, that is whole,
Does the mind fall to rest;
The pearl has grown,
Swollen over the speck of sand,
Button of cream and white silk
Glimmers
At the base of the sea,
Frozen into relief.

155 *Preserve*

No one knows,
Where all the energy grows.
The Earth drinks up remnants
Of old hours spent in the spinning of phrases
And movements, that have turned to stone.
The past is locked up like an old film,
The shapes and feelings all, buried alive
Somewhere
In an invisible archive
Kept to preserve the giving moment,
Which was received
Shrivels into seed
And falls away
To grow again later
Into an explosion,
Black grains
Of giving.

156 *Signs*

There are signs,
Strange to interpret, but there to be found,
If you perceive hard enough.
The link once conceived
Grows daily.
A coincidence that multiplies,
A reversal of upheaval
Into order,
The slots fitting together one by one
Into a geometry of peace.
Moments when all is explained
Not verbally or causally
But simply by the light of the bulbs shining down
Onto a group of people,
As they listen to the silence
Between the rise and fall of their conversation.

157 *Belief*

When it is cold and empty,
Black sky,
Blind eye,
I come to you, Lord, frozen
And know that the tiny black speck in the albumen
Will be nourished
And grow to explosion.

158 *Evolution*

This passage along the days,
Does it lead to a greater knowing?
Nights watched by the stars,
That prick the consciousness
Into moments
Of steel delight.
Would a hundred years release some
Impenetrable source?
Or is it a horizontal journey.
Sailing us along,
Lulled into parallel acquiescence.

159 *Anchor-man*

Anchor-man,
Black as the night you are.
Pulling out your boat further across the sea.
You beckon me;
I saw you once in a dream,
Eyes black as Lethe
Calling me back.
The waves rolled over,
Grey tongues lashing.
I do not know who you serve.
Some God perhaps
Or worse.
The days pass by like balloons on a string,
Bright evenings
Punctured by the night,
And always I seek
A little more
The words I choose to speak.
Black as the night you are,
And as the night I do not know you,
But must rest a while to find you.

160 *Reconciliation*

Uncorrupted, He participated,
Tore off the outer skin.
The arm exposed to feel,
White lymph weeping
Vulnerable
To bridge the gap
Between indignant man and God.
No reconciliation ever complete
We ebb and flow between doubt and understanding
A stab of love in recall of His deed, we endure the smell
Of human involvement.
Then distracted by telephone calls into forgetfulness.

161 *Cave God*

At the bottom of my mind's cave
Lies a wedge of darkness,
And here I retreat,
Hollow of deep mud gloom
With glints of gold-ore
Sparkling from the shadows.
In the silence of the self's core
I drag out the atoms of goodness,
That will redeem me.

God's presence is not a crutch
It is the cave I was born in
And my return to it is natural.
Black shadow God,
Who resides in my empty mind
That sinks slowly to the bottom
And finds peace.

162 *Knowledge*

Only God knows the truth
Of the shades that bind and divide us.
Only he knows our duplicity.
I can deceive you,
And sometimes myself.
You can deceive the world
And sometimes your dreams.
But neither of us can deceive Him.

INDEX OF FIRST LINES

163 *Security*

It does not lie in a house and home,
It does not lie in a mate,
It does not lie in the giving of love,
Nor the absence of conflict and hate.
It lies in the conscious essence of truth,
Which motivates every act,
Resolute selfhood, strong and mature,
Forms a circle, secure and compact.

164 *The Dance*

A ring of friends, arms linked softly
Around supporting shoulders.
Legs curved into a dance
In the heat of orange midnight party lights.
To dance a dance of joy is meaningful,
But this is a dance of rest.
No movement, but the twining of colliding legs,
The slow shuffle and the bony hand,
Which eases the falling arm.
They are supporting each other in the struggle
Against themselves,
Mocking the force, that binds them into a gregarious ring.
Everyone of them would like to ease their way out
Of the tangle of arms and waists and hips,
But the magnet of cushion resting flesh
Is too strong, too linking.
Slowly the circle moves on
And the nodding heads fall together in the centre,
A muted clack.
They smile at the absurdity,
And continue the slow dance of life.

165 *Yellow Flame*

Curiosity infinite
There is much work to be done.
Lest I will never find a destination
But must go
Plaited in three directions
And feel the tangle.
At the end a flame
Flickers yellow.
Gaze joined to the central pulse
No moment will ever be more real than this one
Not before,
Not after.
Now I will go,
Never to reach out of this burnishing
Inside
Yellow flame.

166 *Praise*

God
Spreads his
Warmth and peace
Over the afternoon air.
Now there is much rippling
In transparent golden light of
The sunless bright hours
Between four and five
Praise be to Him,
Who knows how
To release contentment
Into the empty chore,
The laborious action,
Now all things around
Rise up and sing silence.
Like the chirping birds
Outside but frozen into no sound.

167 *Corn Song*

I sang a song of yearning and derision
I sang alone in a field of poppied corn
And the birds stopped singing
And pecking the leafy bushes.
Instead they listened to my song and were intrigued.
The corn-sheaves stretched up high during my singing
To catch the subtle nuances of my meaning.
I sang until my throat began to ache
And the flowers that I was holding
Fluttered to the ground
And my watch stopped ticking,
And the birds started singing
And then I lay down in the corn
And dreamt of poppies.

Epilogue: To Speak

You say everything so explicitly
That the meaning is annihilated.
Words.
What are they but the diminishing of meaning
Into letter-structures?
When our forefathers groaned in caves
And painted blood-red patterns on the rock-walls,
There was no confusion.
So that we may understand each other a little better
Let us keep very silent.
Silent   SSShhh.
SSShhh   Sil—   SShhh.

Index of Poems

Note: this index includes page numbers for poems published in the companion volumes, *Inside the Stretch of My Heart* and *Before and After the Darkness*.

* = this volume.
B = *Before and After the Darkness*
I = *Inside the Stretch of My Heart*

Acorn (I) 113
Acquiescence (I) 223
Adulthood (B) 47
After the Quarrel* 49
Afterwards* 184
Age (I) 103
Ago* 144
Aim, The* 65
Alien* 183
Anchor-man* 206
Ants (B) 60
Apple-Blossom Scent* 24
Ascetic, The (I) 229
Aversion (I) 31
Awakening* 171

Bag, The* 122
Ballad* 73
Ballroom, The* 38
Bank Holiday (I) 85
Beethoven (B) 67
Before and After the Darkness (B) 54
Being* 138
Belief* 204
Between Before and After (B) 38
Bio-Energetics (I) 140
Black and White Universe (B) 488
Black Star* 170
Blackbird* 98
Blind Man, The (I) 67
Blue (B) 29

Bluffer, The (I) 49
Boast, The (I) 59
Bones (I) 91
Bore, The (I) 70
Boredom (I) 95
Brain (I) 182
Bubble (I) 62
Bureaucrat, The (I) 34
Burnt Out by the Shadows* 63
Bus (I) 115

Cactus (I) 121
Call (I) 25
Camera (I) 232
Cave God* 208
Chain (I) 40
Change* 91
Chastity DOS 33
Chawton House* 181
Chicken Bone* 59
Choice, The (I) 186
Christmas Eve (I) 159
Clam* 58
Combat (B) 41
Communication in Silence (I) 41
Concrete Ground* 82
Confession* 47
Conflict* 165
Consolation of Illusion, The (B) 36
Continue* 141
Conviction* 137

217

INDEX OF POEMS

Corn Song* 214
Couple, The* 45
Corrupt* 169
Cotton-Wool Words* 55
Cousins* 28
Cracked Heart (B) 34
Creation* 135
Crocodile (B) 72
Crossed Line (I) 46
Crowd (I) 65
Current of Belief (I) 198
Cut-outs DOS 53
Cycle (I) 240
Cynic (B) 44

Dance, The* 211
Day (I) 23
Day and Night (B) 68
Deaf Ear, The (I) 169
Decision* 151
Deserted (B) 50
Development* 148
Devils* 160
Disillusionment* 88
Display (I) 187
Distrust (I) 184
Divorce (I) 215
Double Biology (I) 109
Double Edged (B) 30
Double Glazing (I) 199
Doubt* 167
Downpour (I) 101
Dragons' Teeth (I) 80
Dream of Oxford (I) 158
Dream of Stairs, The* 76
Dreams Talk (B) 28
Duality* 75
Duel* 161
Dust (I) 42

Earthquake (B) 56
Egg (I) 179
Enemy, The (I) 75
Energy* 138
Ephraim (I) 105

Evening Class, The (I) 133
Evil (I) 195
Evolution* 205
Eyes (I) 206

Façade (I) 197
Facets* 64
Fainting, The (I) 154
Fall (B) 31
Fallen Away (I) 234
Falling* 39
False Image* 69
Fear* 136
Fear of the Lone Self (B) 75
Feathers* 120
Fifty Per Cent (I) 219
Filter (I) 181
Fire (I) 237
Fire Song (B) 69
First Love* 37
Fishes (I) 60
Fishing (I) 93
Flight (I) 125
Flock of Blackbirds, A (I) 79
Food-Time (I) 118
Foretaste (I) 137
Forwards* 191
Four-Leaved (I) 211
Friday Afternoons (I) 83
Frightened of the Night (B) 27
Frost (I) 224
Fulcrum* 106
Future, The (I) 194
Future Nightmare (B) 55

Geometry of the Mind (B) 35
Gift* 57
Giving* 94
God and Satan (I) 191
Gold Door* 193
Grape Picking* 34
Grief* 187
Growth (I) 100
Guilt (B) 40

INDEX OF POEMS

Hard Road, The* 23
Heat* 114
Holocaust* 164
Honesty (B) 23
Hospital in Winter* 86
Housewarming (B) 62
Hum of Silence, The (B) 39
Hunger (I) 117
Hypnosis (I) 139

I Wonder What This Constellation Will
    Be* 190
Illusion* 124
Image (I) 132
Incommunicado (I) 52
Inconsolation* 197
Individuation* 156
Infatuation (B) 42
Infection (I) 221
Insect (I) 165
Insight* 200
Instant (I) 190
Intercom (I) 37
Interior (I) 143
Interruption (I) 84
Interval* 130
Involvement (I) 214
It Will Pass (B) 64

Jealousy (I) 183
Joke, The (I) 69
Journey (I) 24

Keyboard* 107
Kibbutz (I) 71
Killing, The* 46
Kite (B) 45
Knowledge* 209

Label (I) 129
Last Respects (I) 141
Laughter, The* 52
Launderette (I) 43
Lemon (I) 111
Leucotomy* 85

Life Story* 26
Line of Memory, The (I) 200
Living-Room (I) 57
Lizard* 119
Losing, The* 104
Loss (I) 150
Lost Between Stone Basins (I) 102
Lost* 79
Love* 134
Luck (B) 25
Lunch (B) 65
Lunchtime (I) 63

Madwoman, The* 95
Malaise (I) 106
Maternity* 146
Meditating (I) 225
Meditation* 74
Meeting (I) 92
Memories of a Solemn Childhood (B) 66
Memory (I) 178
Midday* 35
Midnight at the Station (I) 152
Misunderstanding (I) 88
Moment (I) 47
Monday Morning (I) 29
Moon-Treasure* 77
Morning Break (I) 44
Morning (I) 28
Mouse (I) 164
Museum Piece (I) 98

Nail Armour* 115
Nature* 143
Needlepoint (I) 210
Neurasthenia* 83
Nice Child* 27
Night (I) 149
Nightmare* 121
Nine to Five-Thirty (I) 33
Ningo Pin, The* 196
No Danger (I) 135
No Further Can I Go (I) 245
No Mother* 147
No Resting Place (I) 220

INDEX OF POEMS

Nocturne * 125
Not to See Him Again (B) 58

Occupational Therapy (I) 231
Off Peak (I) 68
Old Woman (I) 110
On the Steps (I) 97
Onion * 93
Open Door, The * 123
Outsize (I) 74
Over-Exposure (I) 201
Oyster (I) 208

Panorama * 168
Paper Children (I) 39
Parasite (I) 108
Park-Time (I) 86
Parting * 50
Party Games (I) 156
Party Time (I) 155
Passing * 62
Passive Involvement (I) 168
Past, The (B) 21
Peace (I) 247
Percentage * 89
Photo (I) 218
Pier (I) 123
Pity (I) 90
Platform (I) 153
Poet, The (I) 172
Poetry * 126
Portent (I) 51
Praise * 219
Preserve * 202
Preview * 29
Primary School (B) 46
Protection * 41
Psychology (I) 192
Pulse * 140
Puppet * 142

Quarrel, The * 48
Question * 158
Questions and Answers (I) 188
Quick Birth * 25

Rainy Day in the Tourist Season (I) 87
Rat-Race (I) 203
Reading (I) 48
Reality (I) 160
Reality Smiles (B) 18
Reclamation * 166
Reconciliation * 207
Reflector (I) 204
Regeneration * 101
Regret * 90
Rejection * 51
Release * 149
Remember * 70
Reminder (I) 167
Rendezvous, The * 36
Respect for the Elders (I) 227
Restoration * 68
Resurgence * 192
Return * 189
Revelation * 81
Rhythm (B) 63
Roaming (I) 180
Rope * 66
Rosanna (I) 136
Roses * 187
Routine (I) 134

Sacrifice (I) 233
Salt (B) 52
Sanity (I) 193
Sartoris (I) 36
Saturday Afternoon (I) 114
Saturday Night (B) 26
Save This Soul * 195
Scapegoat's Cry, The (I) 185
Schizophrenia * 84
Search, The (I) 170
Security * 210
See-Saw * 105
Selfhood * 128
Separation * 56
Shades (B) 49
Shadows (I) 89
She Searched for Happiness * 182
Shell * 133

INDEX OF POEMS

Shock* 185
Shyness (I) 142
Signs* 203
Silence* 177
Silk-Worm (I) 99
Silver (B) 74
Sin* 80
Singer, The* 113
Six Haikus (I) 226
Six o'clock (I) 124
Skull-Light* 127
Smile* 44
Smile, The (I) 209
Smiled upon a Face (I) 239
Snowdrop (I) 228
Something Is Lost (B) 24
Song of a Schizophrenic Monk* 112
Song of the Crow (I) 235
Sophistication (I) 217
Soul, The* 198
Spellbound* 40
Spider* 129
Spiral of Light* 60
Spur* 163
Squatter, The (B) 61
Stepping Outside (I) 144
Stifled (I) 82
Stones, The (I) 126
Street Dance (I) 81
Success (I) 207
Suicide* 175
Summer (I) 61
Summer Evening (I) 130
Sun on the Track (I) 244
Surprise (I) 145

Talents, The* 150
Teatime (I) 96
Telephone (I) 45
Television (I) 166
Ten Days of Penitence (I) 177
Those Who Do Not Question Much (I) 104
Three Witches (B) 48
Through the Barrier (I) 38

Through the Needle's Eye (B) 22
Tightrope (I) 205
Time (I) 26
Time Frozen (B) 69
Time Machine (I) 94
Time Suspended* 108
Time's Whispering Silence (B) 71
To Create* 19
To Forestall (I) 112
To Grieve* 186
To Speak* 215
To Write (I) 173
Topsy-Turvy (B) 32
Torpor (I) 53
Trafalgar (I) 73
Tree and Leaf (B) 77
Trendy People (I) 138
Tryptich* 157
Tube (I) 131
Tube-Time (I) 32
Tulip (I) 238
Tunnel* 145
Turbulence (I) 196
Twentieth Century* 155
Twins* 162
Two Cures (I) 212
Two o'clock (B) 33
Two Sides (I) 213

Ugliness (I) 58
Ugly, The* 97

Vacuum (I) 72
Verdure (I) 107
View (I) 122
Vision* 103
Vision, The* 111

Waiter, The (I) 119
Waiting, The* 116
Waitress, The (I) 120
Wakening* 102
Waking (I) 27
Wallflower (I) 246
Wandering Through the Days* 61

INDEX OF POEMS

War Baby (I) 230
Wasted Years (I) 222
Water* 172
Water-Bird* 54
Waves* 199
We Follow Our Gods (I) 236
Wedding, The* 67
Weep Before God* 174
Whale (B) 59
Whale Ideas (B) 19
When His Arms Closed Around You* 43
When Morning Is Whiter than Shell (I) 30
When the Door Opens* 194
When the Hands Freeze Cold,* 78
When You Love Someone So Strangely* 42
Why Write? (I) 171
Widow Spider (I) 216
Will (B) 37
Will, The (I) 189
Winter (I) 151
Winter Dampness (B) 17
Worms (I) 50
Writing (I) 174

Yellow Flame* 212
Yoga (I) 163
Yoga Dance* 110

Index of First Lines

Note: this index includes page numbers for poems published in the companion volumes, *Inside the Stretch of My Heart* and *Before and After the Darkness*.
* = this volume.
B = *Before and After the Darkness*
I = *Inside the Stretch of My Heart*

Line	Poem	Book	Page
A flock of blackbirds / They cry and cry	A Flock of Blackbirds	I	79
A frightening thing is memory	Memory	I	178
A glass of water and a tube of	Suicide	*	175
A gratuitous gift / A letter of good fortune	Luck	B	25
A guilt I feel, which is not needed, yet	The Scapegoat's Cry	I	185
A hidden chunk / Vulnerable / When	Reality	I	160
A jade silk-worm in the gallery	Silk-Worm	I	99
A man and a woman in a restaurant	The Joke	I	69
A phone-call from a woman / Who was	Two Sides	I	213
A poem cannot be contrived wilfully	To Create	*	19
A ring of friends, arms linked softly	The Dance	*	211
A shy polythene bag / Keeps the washing	Shyness	I	142
A swarm of birds fly fanlike overhead	Panorama	*	168
A tightrope of people / Every word must	Tightrope	I	205
A typewriter tapping, dust upon my desk	Morning Break	I	44
A wide expanse of gleaming spirals	The Dream of Stairs	*	76
After a long gap between poem / And poem	Writing	I	174
After all this time / Only a brick wall left	Divorce	I	215
After the broad road, / White as a pillar	Dragons' Teeth	I	80
After the cinema / The painted eyes and	Christmas Eve	I	159
After the quarrel / We sat in the night-	After the Quarrel	*	49
After the visitors departed / Slowly from	Yoga	I	163
All digging down to the same roots	Meditating	I	225
All that summer / The trees cracked	First Love	*	37
An all-devouring void inside me bleats	Hunger	I	117
Anchor-man, / Black as the night you are	Anchor-man	*	206
Apple-blossom scent, / Sickly strong	Apple-Blossom Scent	*	24
At certain times of the day / The time of	The Stones	I	126
At one o'clock, / Head swollen to a	Bubble	I	62
At the back of the moon, / Beyond the	Moon-Treasure	*	77
At the bottom of my mind's cave	Cave God	*	208
At the end of the long day / When the	Remember	*	70
At this moment, / I have curved round	Moment	I	47
At three o'clock / The line that cuts the	Roses	*	187
Baby breathing, mother peeping	Development	*	148
Bank holiday Monday white afternoon	Interruption	I	84
Bare carpet peeling off / Soft fluff	The Squatter	B	61

INDEX OF FIRST LINES

Beyond the footlights of the open-air	*Summer Evening*	I	130
Birds singing silver / Outside rain-	*Sartoris*	I	36
Black star / Make me strong / Against	*Black Star*	*	170
Blighted / Earth waved return to its	*Fall*	B	31
Blue aproned lady waddles to and fro	*Teatime*	I	96
Blue cushions / Plumped out	*Living-Room*	I	57
Books dust / Woolly paper at edges	*Tree and Leaf*	B	77
Bonds that break and merge / Day in	*Chain*	I	40
Born to a bellow of music outside the	*Life Story*	*	26
Bought on an impulse, / It cost three days	*The Bag*	*	122
Brown and pink arms / And faces	*Crowd*	I	65
Can it ever be recovered, / Integrity of	*Restoration*	*	68
Can never give enough, / As much as I	*Giving*	*	94
Can you not accept the fact / That I can	*Fifty Per Cent*	I	219
Canniballed / Not aware	*The Past*	B	21
Cannot feel a proper sorrow, / Cannot	*To Grieve*	*	186
Cannot find peace of mind, / Blue sky	*Turbulence*	I	196
Cannot live glad hours all the time	*The Open Door*	*	123
Cannot trust you, / Though know you well	*Distrust*	I	184
Cats spawn kittens. / Sun ties cellophane	*Growth*	I	100
Changed. / The white skin was still the	*Meeting*	I	92
Charcoal drawings / Fading into fibres	*Museum Piece*	I	98
Circle / Shoes in the morning	*The Bureaucrat*	I	34
Cold clatter of feet against the pavement	*Concrete Ground*	*	82
Cold feet on an office afternoon	*Boredom*	I	95
Cotton-wool words, / Cloud-spun	*Cotton-Wool Words*	*	55
Cousins / Are siblings once removed	*Cousins*	*	28
Crack / Between dawn and morning	*Something Is Lost*	B	24
Cricklewood in dust, / Garbage gleaming	*Saturday Afternoon*	I	114
Crisp voice, newly ironed / Along with the	*Memories of a*	B	66
Crossing the road / I though I recognised	*False Image*	*	69
Curiosity infinite / There is much work	*Yellow Flame*	*	212
Curiously / Relieved I stare at the knife	*Six o'clock*	I	124
Cut out with regret, / Pull back into	*Regret*	*	90
Daily routine of / Coil upon coil of	*Nine to Five-Thirty*	I	33
Despair, the whale / Swallow up the	*Whale*	B	59
Discovered / Sucking slowly on a straw	*Midday*	*	35
Do not be dependent upon the one	*Sacrifice*	I	233
Down sticks of rain, / Neck gasping fish	*Downpour*	I	101
Each day month week / We polish shoes	*Rhythm*	B	63
Each one of us / Will one day be broken	*Forwards*	*	191
Endless book of days / Each night	*Journey*	I	24
Ephraim in his bedsitter / Smooths out	*Ephraim*	I	105
Every day / Springs forth twins	*Energy*	*	138
Every time I fall in love / Sharpness of	*Infatuation*	B	42
Everyone must bear between their fingers	*When the Hands...*	*	78
Fallen away / From the old God-love-	*Being*	*	138
Falling short / Compromise / As the air	*Between Before and*	B	38
Fear of motherhood. / A broken glass	*No Mother*	*	147
Five different faculties have we unknowing	*Eyes*	I	206
Fixed / Upon a tulip / I saw / Blue tinged	*Tulip*	I	238

INDEX OF FIRST LINES

First line	Title		Page
Flames and torture-rack of a Tudor epic	Stepping Outside	I	144
Fools / That grin and have faith	Those Who Do Not	I	104
For four years we have worked in the	Communication in	I	41
Force open these eyelids shuttered so	Waking	I	27
Four girls / Sharing gossip / At lunchtime	Lunch	B	65
Frost and fog through the windows	View	I	122
Frozen fingernails turning yellow	Blackbird	*	98
Gilted leaves / That paint the sun	Guilt	B	40
God / Spreads his / Warmth and peace	Praise	*	219
Grey slaps that peel down / To neat shapes	Occupational Therapy	I	231
Hair aflame with the heat, / Eyes	The Reading	I	48
Hatred dwells among people, / Like	Verdure	I	107
He mocked her drawing, / Black criss-	The Killing	*	46
Heart cracked into jagged edges / Like	Cracked Heart	B	34
Heat dissolves me, frees the barriers	Heat	*	114
Her head is cider-swollen to a bubble	No Danger	I	135
Her voice hit the air with a subtle sweep	The Singer	*	113
Hidden in a telephone kiosk / On an	Last Respects	I	141
Hideous jollity / Kipper on the table and	Adulthood	B	47
High above the earth / Upon a tightrope	Rope	*	66
His anger murdered her with eagle eyes	Bones	I	91
His eyes / Black / Will hypnotise	Geometry of the M.	B	35
His moccasins spattered with green mud	The Rendezvous	*	36
His poised / Eyes, / Leaping fish	Fishing	I	93
His writing is more real to him than life.	To Write	I	173
Hot silence / Divides the air / Into good	The Hum of Silence	B	39
Hypocritical / With each change of	Involvement	I	214
I accept this, the stifled past / I can endure	Acquiescence	I	223
I am a child of the twentieth century	Twentieth Century	*	155
I am a puppet, / Jerking one and two and	Puppet	*	142
I am a shell / Catching echoes of the past	Shell	*	133
I am a turnip gone mouldy / And my top	Corrupt	*	169
I am an egg. / A black band in the middle	Egg	I	179
I am frightened of the night / That suckers	Frightened of the N.	B	27
I am one person/Sometimes the snowdrop	Snowdrop	I	228
I am pale and white / Calm and quiet	Chastity	*	33
I can never know you completely	Kite	B	45
I could tear you out of me,	Chicken Bone	*	59
I do not know / Whether I have the	Surprise	I	145
I dreamt I had a tiny ear growing inside my	Future Nightmare	B	55
I felt myself falling through a hole in the	Return	*	189
I have forgotten it, / The guilt which lay	The Losing*		104
I have known you in another life	Shadows	I	89
I have nothing, / Unless I have all	Spur	*	163
I have peeled off the façade	Onion	*	93
I have scrubbed the house from top to	Disillusionment	*	88
I have wilfully flicked an ounce of flesh	Rejection	*	51
I hear an inner thump and must express	Individuation	*	156
I hear time's whispering silence in my ears	Time's Whispering	B	71
I hung upon the splintering beam of oak	Fire Song	B	69
I know a man / Who goes to church every	Crocodile	B	72

INDEX OF FIRST LINES

I lay on the garden hammock / Stared up	Conviction	*	137
I sang a song of yearning and derision	Corn Song	*	214
I see you shadow-bound / Between the	Shades	B	49
I thought of you, picking grapes	The Bore	I	70
I thought she was so cool, so untouchable	Trendy People	I	138
I wish, I wait. I wait and I wish.	Ballad	*	73
I wonder what this constellation will be	I Wonder What This	*	190
I wrote away at ease until the poets	Why Write?	I	171
Id, / Evil id, / Burning cantankerous in	Evil	I	195
Ideas / Like ants / Multiply, swarm and	Ants	B	60
If I could sink down into my stomach	Fulcrum	*	106
If we never see each other again,	Parting	*	50
If you could love the person / Whom you	Combat	B	41
I'll give you a ningo pin, / A pin of God	The Ningo Pin	*	196
In a café by a window / There is no	Vacuum	I	72
In another life / Many transmigrations	Lizard	*	119
In Chawton House, the birthplace of	Chawton House	*	181
In France / The mistletoe sprouts on oak	Parasite	I	108
In me / You stay / White fire	Through the Needle's	B	22
In the antique shop on the corner	Torpor	I	53
In the falling away, / Grey wings of bird	Sin	*	80
In the peak of the rush-hour / The man	Off Peak	I	68
In the tube / At twenty minutes to nine	Tube-Time	I	32
In this Victorian parlour / Eggshell walls	Interior	I	143
Infection / Takes us out of the cardboard	Infection	I	221
Inside my head / Fly / A white bird and	Song of the Crow	I	235
Invisible strings / Sweep the squares	Paper Children	I	39
Is it a nightmare or a dream? / I see	Dream of Oxford	I	158
Is this an eternal waking / After the eye	Afterwards	*	184
It does not lie in a house and home	Security	*	210
'It is rude,' said Alice, 'to make personal	Questions and	I	188
Keats wrote indeed / That when	The Line of Memory	I	200
Knowing how he does not love you	Spiral of Light	*	60
Leap into the white void of Monday	Monday Morning	I	29
Leaves crush branches, / Emerald sting	Cycle	I	240
Let the ugly speak / In angular smiles	The Ugly	*	97
Life is not symmetrical, / A layer of	See-Saw	*	105
Lilting and loving, loving and lilting	The Ballroom	*	38
Lime teeth, / Straw of grass	Kibbutz	I	71
Listening / To the hardy battleaxe	War Baby	I	230
Listening to two conversations at once	Crossed Line	I	46
Lost between stone basins / And lions	Lost Between Stone	I	102
Love, once wanted, / Panacea to blunt	Double Edged	B	30
May / Peace birds trees sway / Welcome	It Will Pass	B	64
Midnight at the station / Shadows	Midnight at the	I	152
Midnight in my square bedsitter	Nocturne	*	125
Morning wakening, / The chalk-white	Wakening	*	102
Mother breaks through / The barriers	Time	I	26
My heart like frozen seaweed hangs	Love	*	134
Nature often belies living experience	Nature	*	143
Net curtains quiver / Like loops of jelly	Two o'clock	B	33

INDEX OF FIRST LINES

No better than the next / We rise and fall	Routine	I	134
No further can I go surely / Than to sink	No Further Can I Go	I	245
No moment will ever be more real than	Through the Barrier	I	38
No one / Can wipe out the fear that is	Fear	*	136
No one knows, / Where all the energy	Preserve	*	202
No security is possible, gateway to your	Gift	*	57
Not to see him again / Never the eyes	Not to See Him	B	58
Now / No love is here / To you / Rolled	No Resting Place	I	220
Now that the pendulum has swung	Time Suspended	*	108
Now that you are thirty / You have	Photo	I	218
Oh black and white machine of information	Television	I	166
On a primrose day in March	Lemon	I	111
On a windy morning in October	Primary School	B	46
On each shoulder is perched an object	Duality	*	75
On the corner of the arcade / Between	Grief	*	187
On the boat pub / Pretentious / Sea curls	Night	I	149
On this afternoon, / Tranquil gold	Maternity	*	146
One man was there / I loved / Face black	Black and White U.	B	43
One soul was lost. / It went tumbling	Tunnel	*	145
Only God knows the truth / Of the	Knowledge	*	209
Our friendship came to nothing, petered	Burnt Out by ...	*	63
Our love, fulfilled, would not be so	Separation	*	56
Out of the barren mind / Flew	Wallflower	I	246
Over the hills / Olive-black trees and	Lost	*	79
Over the morning / Hangs	Portent	I	51
Pain produces logic / To anaesthetise	Roaming	I	180
Parabola of water. / Hoop bent	Water-Bird	*	54
Party games are fun. / Let's throw away	Party Games	I	156
Pass on to the next / It grows	Continue	*	141
Pause, / While London changes	Trafalgar	I	73
Peach row of faces / Frozen into scrutiny	Six Haikus	I	226
People/Cluster like clover in the meadows	Four-Leaved	I	211
Perhaps this daily journal, / Pages of red	The Search	I	170
Pity / Passes through the layered	Pity	I	90
Please believe / That I want nothing	Facets	*	64
Potted plant between the lace of curtains	Cactus	I	121
Problems/That litter the mind like pebbles	Success	I	207
Rat-race, / Squeaks in the running	Rat-Race	I	203
Reality painful / As gasping fish out of	Quick Birth	*	25
Reality smiles, / Does not grow any	Reality Smiles	B	18
Red telephone kiosk / Leaning against	Time Machine	I	94
Respect for the elders, / Is it a tyranny	Respect for the Elders	I	227
Rosanna is silent and blonde and haughty	Rosanna	I	136
Rush-hour malaise. / Slow plodding of	The Blind Man	I	67
Sanity lies in emotional wholeness	Sanity	I	193
Satan grew so bright/That he sparked out	God and Satan	I	191
Saturday night / The broken down fire	Saturday Night	B	26
Save this soul / Catch its dropping	Save This Soul	*	195
Scorching light of day / White fire	Morning	I	28
Scrawny blue-veined hand still clutching	Old Woman	I	110
Sharpen the brain / To a fine point of	Brain	I	182

227

INDEX OF FIRST LINES

She laughed. 'I looked out of the window	Twins	*	162
She searched for happiness / As if it were	She Searched for	*	182
She slept in a chair by the table	Dreams Talk	B	28
She speaks glibly of intellectual despair	Cynic	B	44
She wants to be happy. / Her voice is	Façade	I	197
Silently, as the days pass, / We wait for	Oyster	I	208
Sitting at twin tables / I see	Fishes	I	60
Sleep in wonder. / Do not know where	Interval	*	130
Slowly the evil / Has seeped into my soul	The Ten Days of	I	177
Slowly the sweet-sour juice trickling	Grape Picking	*	34
Slowly / Unfolds / White salt peace	Peace	I	247
Smile upon us, lazy beauty, / Out of	The Vision	*	111
Smiled upon a face / That offered nothing	Smiled upon a Face	I	239
So I survived and compromised with	Regeneration	*	101
So many gaps, / White patches, which	Percentage	*	89
So many things given / Mornings that	Deserted	B	50
Some eagle hovers overhead	Call	I	25
Something / Of Hell / I saw / With this	Foretaste	I	137
Standing in the black rain	Passing	*	62
Stay attuned to the forces of life	Pulse	*	140
Strange to see this familiar face	Dust	I	42
Strength of you / Crag of shoulder	Honesty	B	23
Stretched out in a darkened room	Vision	*	103
Sun on the track / Three rods of fire	Sun on the Track	I	244
Sunday afternoon. / Out of the glass-	Park-Time	I	86
Sunday afternoon, / White as salt	Salt	B	52
Sunday television, an Italian wartime	Reminder	I	167
Sunflayed, / Cross-kneed upon steps	On the Steps	I	97
Take a petal, imprint it on your mind	Meditation	*	74
Taken by surprise / I squirm	Food-Time	I	118
Ten years ago they sat together at a	The Wedding	*	67
Tepid afternoon tea-leaf tea / Fills	Stifled	I	82
The birds wing jerkily across the mauve	Flight	I	125
The black days, / Metallic white sky	The Waiting	*	116
The boast / Spilled out of my lips	The Boast	I	59
The book of my mind lies open	Schizophrenia	*	84
The broken-down fire / Fuses the flat	Ago	*	144
The bus is swamped with raincoats	Bus	I	115
The cat, a seething kettle, / Paws and	Aversion	I	31
The challenge of an enemy	The Enemy	I	75
The coach is flashing through the hills	Misunderstanding	I	88
The consolation of illusion / Love and	Consolation of I.	B	36
The crazy sect are dancing / Along	Street Dance	I	81
The criminal is ill, / Steals in surprise	Topsy-Turvy	B	32
The daddy long legs / Cannot scuttle	Insect	I	165
The day I put away the tranquillisers	Awakening	*	171
The day slips across the murmuring sea of	Day and Night	B	68
The death of someone you love	Inconsolation	*	197
The earth turns rebel against itself	Day	I	23
The empty spaces and wasted days	Resurgence	*	192
The essence of goodness / However	The Will	I	189

INDEX OF FIRST LINES

The falling in love down through a hole	Falling	*	39
The fat shopper in the fitting-room	Outsize	I	74
The first time I glimpsed Hell	Preview	*	29
The girl in purple trousers lay on the	Release	*	149
The girl sways her pregnant hips	Earthquake	B	56
The girl with the operated nose	Change	*	91
The God in my head is more real	Skull-Light	*	127
The green eyes of the black tomcat	Jealousy	I	183
The half people / Who live cramped days	Frost	I	224
The human soul floats down from	The Soul	*	198
The laughter grew / Into gold coils	The Laughter	*	52
The Man on the Cross, He rose	Question	*	158
The mouse / A tiny grey ball of fur	Mouse	I	164
The park on Easter Monday	Bank Holiday	I	85
The party was a slit of light under the door	Party Time	I	155
The person who knows you well	Display	I	187
The pigeon coos mercilessly / Outside	Intercom	I	37
The poet looks out / Of his head / Sieves	The Poet	I	172
The pounding Beethoven, / Beats	The Deaf Ear	I	169
The railway line of life / Never to be	To Forestall	I	112
The silence has been broken / By a string	The Evening Class	I	133
The smile, / A long-remembered habit	The Smile	I	209
The snow is falling February white	Hospital in Winter	*	86
The soul searcher / Lays aside his pen	Conflict	*	165
The spirit entered them; / Salt smoking	Insight	*	200
The Stoic / Thickens his skin with oil	Two Cures	I	212
The telephone / Black furry ear	Telephone	I	45
The torn fingernail, which you will pull	Nail Armour	*	115
The Tube on a Saturday evening	Tube	I	131
The washing-machine's stomach	Launderette	I	43
The wasted years / Thrown down a well	Wasted Years	I	222
The waves roll in / Day after day	Waves	*	199
The will frittered out / Would not obey	Will	B	37
There are signs, / Strange to interpret	Signs	*	203
There is a gold door in the sky	Gold Door	*	193
There is a madwoman gaunt and brown	The Madwoman	*	95
There is a test-card C of selfhood	Keyboard	*	107
'There is an answer to every problem	Holocaust	*	164
There is no cure for being one person	Selfhood	*	128
There was the first man / And the first	Fallen Away	I	234
They are mocking the devils within me	Doubt	*	167
They cut a slice out of the brain,	Leucotomy	*	85
They didn't mean to quarrel.	The Quarrel	*	48
They scrub the drawers / And sweep	Housewarming	B	62
They spoke blunt friendship / And their	Widow Spider	I	216
Things are not so easy for you now, my love	Before and After	B	54
Thinking is away from the grain	Blue	B	29
Thirst. / A crystal glass ball of ice-cold	Water	*	172
This death / I cannot quite believe in	Shock	*	185
This dismembered leg / From an ancient	Age	I	103
This hypnotist / Has a sandalwood voice	Spellbound	*	40

229

INDEX OF FIRST LINES

This park greenery / Overwhelms	Fear of the Lone Self	B	75
This passage along the days, / Does it	Evolution	*	205
This restaurant is like a fore-echo	The Waiter	I	119
Three words. / Brief answer to his	Incommunicado	I	52
Through a forest of taboos and ill-fortune	Needlepoint	I	210
Through bleary lattice-work of rain	Rainy Day in the	I	87
Through the railings, / Beyond the rail-	Platform	I	153
Thursday afternoons are for double	Double Biology	I	109
Tightening threads break through	Over-Exposure	I	201
Time frozen into ice-drops / Clings quietly	Time Frozen	B	70
Tired of pure thoughts, crisp, snowflake	Current of Belief	I	198
To be loved / Is to stop thinking	Protection	*	41
To hear sometimes the grey groan of	Tryptich	*	157
To pay back in energy / The gift I have	The Talents	*	150
To run into a long tunnel, blackness	Poetry	*	126
To wake up from a three o'clock	Nightmare	*	121
Today, / Floating on an eiderdown of	Feathers	*	120
Try to absorb / The news on television	Passive Involvement	I	168
Twin pawns of ivory on a chessboard	Duel	*	161
Two decades and a half have passed	Creation	*	135
Uncorrupted, He participated, / Tore off	Reconciliation	*	207
Unlike the gypsy in the tent with a glass	The Future	I	194
Untidy Friday afternoons, / Ends of	Friday Afternoons	I	83
Virginia saw it too, / The door	Neurasthenia	*	83
Walking away from the doctor's	Malaise	I	106
Walking between the great stone	Image	I	132
Walking one by one / Down the white	Lunchtime	I	63
Walking over the grass on an evening in	Label	I	129
Walking, windswept / Over the slatted	Pier	I	123
Wallflowers scorching blood in July	Summer	I	61
Wandering through the days	Wandering ...	*	61
Warm, friendly voice, / Cultivated	Sophistication	I	217
We follow our gods / Doggedly	We Follow Our Gods	I	236
We lay in a circle on the carpet, heads	Hypnosis	I	139
We live in the age of psychology	Psychology	I	192
We met on a blistering summer's	Ugliness	I	58
We sat in the damp evening air	Confession	*	47
We were talking in a hut on a strange	The Bluffer	I	49
Weep before God / When the ice breaks	Weep Before God	*	174
Whale ideas / Blubber home	Whale Ideas	B	19
What is the use of this strained sensibility	Song of a...	*	112
When all the love has dwindled away	Acorn	I	113
When his arms closed around you	When His Arms...	*	43
When I tore away the curtain of my	Revelation	*	81
When I was a child, a naughty child	Nice Child	*	27
When I was fifteen, / I stood in front of	Devils	*	160
When I was young and the rain poured	Worms	I	50
When it is cold and empty, / Black sky	Belief	*	204
When morning is whiter than shell	When Morning Is	I	30
When my anger broods and stirs	Three Witches	B	48
When the dog ran away in the middle of	Loss	I	150

INDEX OF FIRST LINES

When the door opens, / The silence will	When the Door	*	194
When the pain comes / Gold spots upon	The Fainting	I	154
When the pain rings true, / Like charnel	Instant	I	190
When we met, / Cardboard figures	Cut-outs	*	53
When you love someone so strangely	When You Love...	*	42
Where the will lies / Flicker to the right	Decision	*	151
White dots in the air / That fizzle	Silence	*	177
Who loves the grey tent of darkness	Winter	I	151
'Why do you smile all the time'	Smile	*	44
Why, when I look at silver, / Can I not see	Silver	B	74
Will eat / Only the bitter flesh of apple	Ascetic, The	I	229
Winter dampness is a fungus	Winter Dampness	B	17
Wish to be reclaimed by the Spirit	Reclamation	*	166
Without the selectivity / Of a brain filter	Filter	I	181
Yoga dance, / Fly away to the north and	Yoga Dance	*	110
You are a non-person. / You do not have	Reflector	I	204
You are a spider flashing out silks,	Spider	*	129
You can try / For a minute, for an hour	The Aim	*	65
You hate my barren mind / And long for	Camera	I	232
You have chosen the hard road	The Hard Road	*	23
You know I feel for you, / Your every	Clam	*	58
You lay above me cutting off the blue	The Couple	*	45
You saved my life with your rock love	The Choice	I	186
You say everything so explicitly	To Speak	*	215
You teach me how to plumb the depths of	Beethoven	B	67
You think you made a precise and unusual	Double Glazing	I	199
You turn your loves into gods / Pillars	Fire	I	237
You, who dwell in a cold and Nordic	Alien	*	183
You work long, steaming days here	The Waitress	I	120
You would like me better / If the grey	Illusion	*	124
Zany clown, / Red velvet jeans stretching	Bio-Energetics	I	140

231

www.ingramcontent.com/pod-product-compliance
Lightning Source LLC
LaVergne TN
LVHW041614070426
835507LV00008B/223